A Walsingham Prayer Book

Elizabeth Ruth Obbard is the novice mistress at the Carmel of Walsingham in Norfolk. She is the author of a number of books which she has also illustrated, including *The History and Spirituality of Walsingham* and *See How I Love You – Meditations on the Way of the Cross with Julian of Norwich*, both published by The Canterbury Press Norwich.

A Walsingham Prayer Book

Compiled by

Elizabeth Ruth Obbard ODC

CANTERBURY
PRESS
Norwich

L242·8

Acknowledgements

Psalms are from the Grail version, © The Grail and published by
Collins in 1963.

Intercessions are from the Roman Breviary, published by Collins
in 1974, © the hierarchies of Australia, England and Wales, and
Ireland. Used with permission.

The passages by Julian of Norwich are from *The Revelations of
Divine Love*, translated by Josef Pichler and used with permission.

Cover photo: Judith Leckie ODC and Louis Quail

© in this compilation Elizabeth Ruth Obbard ODC 1997

First published 1997 by The Canterbury Press Norwich
(a publishing imprint of Hymns Ancient & Modern Limited
a registered charity)
St Mary's Works, St Mary's Plain,
Norwich, Norfolk, NR3 3BH

Elizabeth Ruth Obbard has asserted her right under the
Copyright, Designs and Patents Act, 1988, to be identified as
Author of this Work

British Library Cataloguing in Publication Data

A catalogue record for this book is available
from the British Library

ISBN 1–85311–170–8

*Typeset by David Gregson Associates, Beccles, Suffolk and
printed and bound in Great Britain by
St Edmundsbury Press Limited, Bury St Edmunds, Suffolk*

In memory of
Mother Inez of the Trinity ODC
and Mother Catherine Clancy RC
Two valiant women

and for Daniel

God then summoned the Archangel
   Holy Gabriel – him He sent
To the Blessed Virgin Mary
   To obtain the Maid's consent.

She consented: in that instant
   The mysterious work was done,
And the Trinity a body
   Wrought and fashioned for the Son.

In this wondrous operation,
   Though the Sacred Three concurred,
He Who in the womb of Mary
   Was Incarnate, is the Word.

He Who had a Father only
   Had a Mother to embrace.
But it was in other fashion
   Than the manner of our race.

In the womb of Holy Mary
   He His flesh did then receive:
So the Son of God Most Highest
   We the Son of Man believe.

St John of the Cross

Walsingham Village

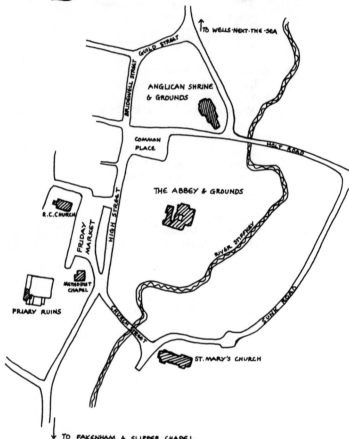

TO WELLS·NEXT·THE·SEA

GUILD STREET

BRIDGEWELL STREET

ANGLICAN SHRINE & GROUNDS

COMMON PLACE

HOLT ROAD

THE ABBEY & GROUNDS

R.C.CHURCH

FRIDAY MARKET

HIGH STREET

RIVER STIFFKEY

METHODIST CHAPEL

PRIARY RUINS

SUNK ROAD

CHURCH STREET

ST. MARY'S CHURCH

↓ TO FAKENHAM & SLIPPER CHAPEL

Contents

1

Walsingham – A Place of Pilgrimage and Prayer

In the year 1061, so the story goes, the widow Richeldis de Favarches, lady of the manor of Little Walsingham, asked Our Lady how she could show honour to her in some special way. In answer to this prayer, Mary led Richeldis in spirit to Nazareth, and pointed out to her the house in which she had received the angel's message that she was chosen to be the Mother of God.

Mary told Richeldis to take the measurements of the house and build another one just like it in Walsingham. It would be a place where people could come to honour Mary and her Son, remembering especially the mystery of the Annunciation and Mary's joyful 'Yes' to conceiving the Saviour.

Richeldis immediately set about erecting a small wooden chapel measuring twenty-three feet six inches by twelve feet ten inches, in accordance with Our Lady's instructions. She loved to pray there, remembering the first holy house at Nazareth and Jesus' growing years in an ordinary family home.

Before departing for the Holy Land, which had recently been opened up by the Crusades, the widow's son, Geoffrey, left his mother's precious chapel in the care of a priest-guardian. He wanted it to be safely preserved, since Mary herself had asked for it. Later a community of Augustinian canons established themselves on the site and enclosed the original wooden house within their great priory church. A statue of Our Lady with the Child on her knee was set up in a place of honour, showing Mary 'at home' in her own dwelling.

Soon pilgrims began to come and pray in the holy house, not only from the area around Walsingham but from all over England and even abroad. Many kings and queens came on pilgrimage and left rich gifts. Thanks to Our Lady of Walsingham, England became known as Mary's Dowry, so much did the people of this land show their love and honour for the Mother of God. On big feasts the holy house would be lit up by hundreds of candles as pilgrims came to pray. It was as if Nazareth were here again in England. Here Our Lady was specially present, and her Son showed mercy to the many sick and needy people who came to ask for help and blessings. All through the Middle Ages Walsingham was a well-known and much-frequented centre of pilgrimage, second only to the Holy Land itself, Rome and Compostella.

In 1538, with the Dissolution of the Monasteries, the Shrine was destroyed and the statue of Our Lady was burned at Smithfield. The holy house was levelled to the ground and the beautiful priory church was left to fall into ruins. Most people forgot that there had been anything special about this quiet Norfolk village, which had once known a constant stream of pilgrims coming to the chapel which had been erected by the widow Richeldis so long ago.

Then in 1875 the Pynson Ballad, a poem telling the story of the foundation of Walsingham, was discovered and printed. Interest in Our Lady of Walsingham was thus revived among both Anglicans and Roman Catholics. The Catholics of the area built a replica of the holy house in miniature for the Church of the Annunciation at King's Lynn (the parish in which Walsingham was situated at that time). In 1897 they held the first pilgrimage since the Reformation to the place where the ancient Slipper Chapel had been purchased and restored by Miss Charlotte Boyd. However, for the time being King's Lynn remained the centre of devotion and the Slipper Chapel stood well cared for but empty.

Meanwhile a new vicar, Alfred Hope Patten, was appointed to the living of Walsingham in 1921. He was determined to reawaken a love for Our Lady in Mary's own village. He had a statue made for the parish church of St Mary according to the pattern on the original Walsingham priory seal. This shows Mary seated on a high-backed throne, holding a lily sceptre, while on her lap sits the Child with the book of the Gospels in his hand. This statue of Our Lady of Walsingham, the first to be made since the original had been destroyed, was installed in the Guild's Chapel of the Anglican parish church on 16 July 1922. Parishioners began to gather there each evening to pray the rosary and offer other prayers of intercession, and the custom of Shrine Prayers has never lapsed since that time.

In 1931 a separate shrine church was erected, and within it was placed a holy house similar to the one made by Richeldis, but this time built of brick and stone rather than wood. The statue was carried there in procession and enthroned above the altar.

Around the same time the Slipper Chapel, located one mile outside the village, was reopened and began to be used for worship by Roman Catholic pilgrims. An additional chapel was dedicated to the Holy Spirit, and in 1982 the beautiful Chapel of Reconciliation, patterned on a Norfolk barn, was built to accommodate the growing number of pilgrims. The Slipper Chapel, like the Anglican shrine, has a statue of Our Lady in a place of honour, carved according to the medieval seal design. The Slipper Chapel has been designated as the National Catholic Shrine of Our Lady in England.

The site of the Augustinian priory is in private hands, but the great east window of the priory church is still standing, and the site of Richeldis' holy house is marked for pilgrims to see. Walsingham has once again become Mary's own village. It is a place saturated with prayer, a place where pilgrims are invited, as of old, to say their personal 'Yes' to God, in union with Mary at the Annunciation.

This prayer book will take you round the special places in Walsingham. It can be used in all or any of them. It can also be used in your own home, where you can make a spiritual pilgrimage to England's Nazareth any time you wish.

Walsingham is 'home from home'. It is Mary's own village and shrine. She invites us to pray with her and live with her as mother, sister, friend and her Son's most perfect disciple.

2

Prayers Before Setting Out on a Pilgrimage

Going on pilgrimage is a very old religious custom. The Jews went up to Jerusalem on pilgrimage every year, and we know that Jesus himself went too, first with Mary and Joseph and later with his disciples. Through the centuries the Holy Land has always been a country sacred to Christians who have wanted to walk in the footsteps of Jesus, but there have also been shrines and other holy places where people have gone to pray and where Mary and the saints have been specially venerated. Walsingham is such a place, and Christians still want to go there to remember the wondrous mystery of God becoming man through the consent of a woman, Mary.

These prayers for a journey can be used before setting out as a reminder that, while a pilgrimage should be a happy and relaxing time, it is also a time of prayer and an opportunity to draw closer to the God who walks with us at every stage of our life's journey.

Psalm 138

V. Our help is in the Name of the Lord.
R. Who made heaven and earth.
V. Watch over all who travel.
R. May your holy angels guard them and keep them safe.

O Lord, you search me and you know me,
you know my resting and my rising,
you discern my purpose from afar.
You mark when I walk or lie down,
all my ways lie open to you.

Response (*R.*): *Lead me, Lord, in the path of life eternal.*

Before ever a word is on my tongue
you know it, O Lord, through and through.
Behind and before you besiege me,
your hand ever laid upon me.
Too wonderful for me is this knowledge,
too high beyond my reach. *R.*

O where can I go from your spirit,
or where can I flee from your face?
If I climb the heavens you are there.
If I lie in the grave you are there. *R.*

If I take the wings of the dawn
and dwell at the sea's furthest end,
even there your hand would lead me,
your right hand would hold me fast. *R.*

If I say, 'Let the darkness hide me
and the light around me be night,'
even darkness is not dark for you
and the night is as clear as the day. *R.*

For it was you who created my being,
knit me together in my mother's womb.
I thank you for the wonder of my being,
for the wonders of all your creation. *R.*

Already you knew my soul,
my body held no secret from you
when I was being fashioned in secret
and moulded in the depths of the earth. *R.*

Your eyes saw all my actions,
they were all of them written in your book;
every one of my days was decreed
before one of them came into being. *R.*

To me how mysterious your thoughts,
the sum of them not to be numbered!
If I count them they are more than the sand;
to finish I must be eternal like you. *R.*

O search me, God, and know my heart.
O test me and know my thoughts.
See that I follow not the wrong path
and lead me in the path of life eternal. *R.*

Let us pray

Heavenly Father, protector of those who trust in you, you
led your people in safety through the desert and brought
them to a land of plenty. Guide us who begin our journey.
Fill us with your Spirit of love. Preserve us from all harm
and bring us safely to our destination.

 May the Lord Jesus be with us to defend us, within us to
keep us, before us to lead us, behind us to guard us, above
us to bless us. And we ask this through the same Christ our
Lord, who lives and reigns with you and the Holy Spirit,
God for ever and ever. Amen.

✝ The Lord bless us and keep us,
the Lord make his face to shine upon us,
the Lord lift up his countenance upon us
and give us peace. Amen.

Prayer before a spiritual pilgrimage

O Jesus, I am a pilgrim on life's road. Be my companion on the way. May I walk with you in ever deeper intimacy, listening to all you have to say to me.

May I journey in spirit, too, with all who are on pilgrimage to Walsingham at this moment, especially those who are laden with a burden of sorrow, pain or suffering. May I carry them in my heart before you with prayer and love.

I think of all the people who have travelled the pilgrim path down the ages, and how Walsingham is saturated with prayer, praise and sacrifice. This way has seen saints and sinners bound together as one in your mystical body, with Mary as their inspiration and model.

Let all who are at the Shrine rediscover a sense of human solidarity and support. Let each care for the other, and let each one know the joy and security of being 'at home' in Mary's Nazareth.

I unite my prayers with those of all pilgrims, offering to you each one with his or her secret joys, sorrows, guilt, fears, sins.

I pray for those struggling with secret sins; those who have ceased to practise their faith because of past hurts; those with marital problems; those who bear a heavy cross without friends to support them and share the burden.

I bring you the whole world, knowing that your Cross and your love are more powerful than the powers of darkness. O Jesus, be always our strength and protection. Amen.

3

Common Prayers

The sign of the Cross

In the name of the Father and of the Son and of the Holy Spirit. Amen.

The Apostles' Creed

I believe in God, the Father almighty, creator of heaven and earth, and in Jesus Christ, his only Son, our Lord, who was conceived by the Holy Spirit, born of the Virgin Mary, suffered under Pontius Pilate, was crucified, died, and was buried. He descended into hell. The third day he rose again from the dead. He ascended into heaven, and sitteth at the right hand of God the Father almighty. From thence he shall come to judge the living and the dead. I believe in the Holy Spirit, the holy Catholic Church, the Communion of Saints, the forgiveness of sins, the resurrection of the body, and life everlasting. Amen.

Our Father

Our Father, who art in heaven,
hallowed be thy name;
thy kingdom come;
thy will be done on earth as it is in heaven.
Give us this day our daily bread;
and forgive us our trespasses,
as we forgive those who trespass against us;
and lead us not into temptation,
but deliver us from evil.
Amen.

Hail Mary

Hail Mary, full of grace, the Lord is with thee,
blessed art thou among women and blessed is the fruit of
thy womb, Jesus.
Holy Mary, mother of God, pray for us sinners,
now and at the hour of our death. Amen.

Glory be to the Father

Glory be to the Father, and to the Son, and to the Holy
Spirit,
As it was in the beginning, is now and ever shall be, world
without end. Amen.

The Angelus

V. The angel of the Lord declared unto Mary.
R. And she conceived by the Holy Spirit.

Hail Mary ...

V. Behold the handmaid of the Lord.
R. Be it done unto me according to thy word.

Hail Mary ...

V. And the Word was made flesh.
R. And dwelt among us.

Hail Mary ...

V. Pray for us, O holy mother of God.
R. That we may be made worthy of the promises of Christ.

Let us pray

Pour forth, we beseech thee, O Lord, thy grace into our
hearts,
that we to whom the Incarnation of Christ thy Son was
made known by the message of an angel,

may by his passion and cross be brought to the glory of his Resurrection.
Through Christ our Lord, Amen.

Regina Coeli (during the Easter season)

Queen of heaven rejoice. Alleluia!
The Son whom it was your privilege to bear. Alleluia!
Has risen as he said. Alleluia!
Pray to God for us. Alleluia!
Rejoice and be glad, Virgin Mary. Alleluia!
For the Lord has truly risen. Alleluia!

Let us pray

O God, you were pleased to give joy to the world through the resurrection of your Son, our Lord Jesus Christ. Grant that through the intercession of the Virgin Mary his mother, we too may come to possess the joys of life everlasting. Through the same Christ our Lord. Amen.

The Memorare

Remember, O most gracious Virgin Mary, that never was it known that anyone who ever fled to your protection, implored your help or sought your intercession, was left unaided. Inspired by this confidence, I fly to you, O Virgin of virgins, my mother. To you I come, before you I stand, sinful and sorrowful. O Mother of the Word Incarnate, despise not my petitions, but in your mercy hear and answer me. Amen.

A form of morning offering

O Jesus, through the most pure heart of Mary,
I offer you all the prayers, works, sufferings and joys of this day,
for all the intentions of your Sacred Heart,
and in union with all the Masses being said throughout the whole world. Amen.

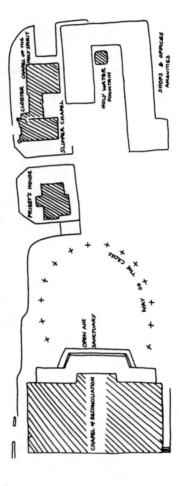

HOLY MILE ⟵ ➝ TO WALSINGHAM VILLAGE

CLOISTER CHAPEL OF THE HOLY SPIRIT

SLIPPER CHAPEL

HOLY WATER FOUNTAIN

SHOPS & OFFICES AMENITIES

PRIEST'S HOUSE

WAY OF THE CROSS

OPEN AIR SANCTUARY

CHAPEL OF RECONCILIATION

GROUNDS of the SLIPPER CHAPEL R.C. SHRINE

4

The Slipper Chapel

The Slipper Chapel was built sometime around 1338 and is dedicated to St Catherine of Alexandria, patron saint of pilgrims. It was constructed in such a way that the sun rises directly behind the altar on her feast day, 25 November.

Here, in medieval times, the pilgrims would confess their sins, then remove their shoes and walk the last 'Holy Mile' into Walsingham barefoot. Henry VIII presumably stopped here when he was en route to Walsingham to give thanks to Our Lady for the birth of a son in January 1511. Unfortunately the child died in February of the same year, and it was Henry who was later responsible for the Shrine's destruction.

After the Dissolution of the Monasteries the Slipper Chapel fell into disrepair, being used as a private dwelling and later as a cow barn. It was purchased and restored by Miss Charlotte Boyd in 1894 and was given to the Benedictines of Downside,

but no services were permitted to be held there. However, in 1930 the new Bishop of Northampton took an interest in the chapel and had it refurbished and decorated in medieval English style. It was opened officially in 1934, since when it has become the national Marian Shrine for the Catholic Church in England.

The altar, richly carved and painted by a local artist, Lilian Dagless, shows St Lawrence (one of the patrons of the ancient Walsingham priory) and St Catherine of Alexandria. The statue of Our Lady of Walsingham, to the left of the altar and under a high canopy, is the focus of devotion.

The Litany of Our Lady of Walsingham

Our Lady of Walsingham, pray to the Lord for us.
Mary conceived without sin, pray to the Lord for us.
Mary the Virgin, pray to the Lord for us.
Mary the Mother of God, pray to the Lord for us.
Mary taken up into Heaven, pray to the Lord for us.
Mary at Bethlehem, pray for all mothers.
Mary at Nazareth, pray for all families.
Mary at Cana, pray for all married couples.
Mary who stood by the Cross, pray for all who suffer.
Mary in the Upper Room, pray for all who wait.
Mary, model of Womanhood, pray for all women.

Woman of faith, keep us in mind.
Woman of hope, keep us in mind.
Woman of charity, keep us in mind.
Woman of suffering, keep us in mind.
Woman of anxiety, keep us in mind.
Woman of humility, keep us in mind.
Woman of purity, keep us in mind.
Woman of obedience, keep us in mind.

Woman who wondered, remember us to God.
Woman who listened, remember us to God.

Woman who followed him, remember us to God.
Woman who longed for him, remember us to God.
Woman who loves him, remember us to God.

Mother of God, be our mother always.
Mother of the Church, be our mother always.
Mother of the World, be our mother always.
Mother whom we need, be our mother always.
Mother who went on believing, we thank God for you.
Mother who never lost hope, we thank God for you.
Mother who loved to the end, we thank God for you.

All holy and ever-living God, in giving us Jesus Christ to be
our Saviour and Brother, you gave us Mary, his Mother, to
be our Mother also; grant, we pray you, that we may be
worthy of so great a Brother and so dear a Mother. May we
come at last to you, the Father of us all, through Jesus Christ
your Son, who lives and reigns with you and the Holy Spirit
for ever and ever. Amen.

Commendation

Jesus, Mary and Joseph, I give you my heart and soul.
Jesus, Mary and Joseph, assist me in my last agony.
Jesus, Mary and Joseph, may I breathe forth my soul in
   peace with you.

(From the Litany by the late Father Eric Doyle OFM)

A personal fiat prayer

Mary, teach me too to say 'Yes,
I am the handmaid of the Lord,
Let all he wills be done in me.
May his Spirit overshadow me, his love be fruitful in me,
his joy abound in my heart.'
Let there be no 'Yes, but ...'
which is really a cover for 'No'.
Let it all be 'Yes,' plain and simple,
a 'Yes' spoken in trust to the One who is eternally faithful.
   Amen.

O Holy Virgin

O Holy Virgin, in the midst of your days of glory, do not
     forget the sorrows of this earth.
Cast a merciful glance upon those who are struggling
     against difficulties, those who are suffering,
with their lips constantly pressed against life's bitter cup.
Have pity on those who love each other and are sepa-
     rated.
Have pity on our rebellious hearts. Have pity on our weak
     faith.
Have pity on those we love. Have pity on those who
     weep, on those who pray, on those who fear.
Grant hope and peace to all. Amen.

Abbe Perreyve

Virgin-born, we bow before thee

Virgin-born, we bow before thee:
Blessed was the womb that bore thee;
     Mary, Mother meek and mild,
     Blessed was she in her Child.
Blessed was the breast that fed thee;
Blessed was the hand that led thee;
     Blessed was the parent's eye
     That watched thy slumbering infancy.

Blessed she by all creation,
Who brought forth the world's salvation,
     And blessed they – for ever blest,
     Who love thee most and serve thee best.
Virgin-born, we bow before thee:
Blessed was the womb that bore thee;
     Mary, Mother meek and mild,
     Blessed was she in her Child.

Reginald Heber

5

The Chapel of the Holy Spirit

The Chapel of the Holy Spirit, together with its sacristies, was built in 1938 and is connected to the Slipper Chapel by a short cloister. It has been completely redesigned as a chapel for the burning of candles and lights in honour of Our Lady. The focal point is a fine mosaic of Mary in the midst of the apostles on the day of Pentecost.

Mary, as Mother of the Church, prays with us, for us, as one of us, that we too may be filled with the Spirit of Jesus and be ready to proclaim his Name to others.

Prayer to the Holy Spirit

Come Holy Spirit, fill the hearts of your faithful
And enkindle in them the fire of your love.

V. Send forth your Spirit and they shall be created,
R. And you shall renew the face of the earth.

Let us pray

Father, with the coming of the Holy Spirit you send new light, new fire, into believing hearts. Grant that we also, receiving the same Holy Spirit, may ever delight in his wisdom and radiate his joy. Through Christ our Lord. Amen.

The secret of sanctity

I am going to reveal to you the secret of sanctity and happiness. Every day, for five minutes, control your imagination and close your eyes to the things of sense, and your ears to all the noises of the world, in order to enter into yourself. Then, in the sanctuary of your baptized soul (which is the temple of the Holy Spirit) speak to that Divine Spirit, saying to him:

'O Holy Spirit, beloved of my soul, I adore you. Enlighten me, guide me, strengthen me, console me, tell me what I should do … Give me your orders. I promise to submit myself to all that you desire of me and to accept all that you permit to happen to me. Let me only know your will.'

If you do this, your life will flow along happily, serenely, and full of consolation even in the midst of trials. Grace will be proportioned to the trial, giving you the strength to carry it, and you will arrive at the gate of Paradise laden with merit. This submission to the Holy Spirit is the secret of sanctity.

Cardinal Mercier

Come Holy Spirit

Come Holy Spirit, and send forth from heaven the radiance of your light,
Come, Father of the poor, come giver of gifts, come light of hearts,
Best Consoler, sweet guest of the soul, sweet refreshment,
In labour rest, coolness in heat, comfort in tears.
O most blessed light, fill the inmost hearts of your faithful;

Without your divine power, nothing is in us except what is
    harmful.
Cleanse what is soiled, water what is dry, heal what is
    wounded;
Bend what is rigid, chafe what is cold, straighten what is
    crooked.
Grant to your faithful who trust in you your sacred seven-
    fold gift,
Grant the reward of virtue, grant at the end salvation,
    grant everlasting joy. Amen.

Prayer of St Mary Magdalen de Pazzi

Come, Holy Spirit. May the union of the Father and the will
of the Son come to us.

You, Spirit of Truth, are the reward of the saints, the
refreshment of souls, the riches of the poor, the treasury of
lovers, the satisfaction of the hungry, the consolation of the
pilgrim Church. You are the One in whom all treasures are
contained.

Come, you who, descending into Mary, caused the Word
to take flesh; effect in us by grace all you accomplished in
her by grace and by nature.

Come, you who are the nourishment of all chaste
thoughts, the fountain of all mercy, the summit of all purity.

Come and take away from us all that hinders us from
being absorbed in you. Amen.

Mary of Nazareth

Mary of Nazareth, sing your song in me.
Open me to the Spirit that he may breathe through me,
and that I may take the music of love wherever I go.
    Amen.

Discendi, amor santo

Come down, O love divine,
Seek thou this soul of mine,
And visit it with thine own ardour glowing;

O comforter, draw near,
Within my heart appear,
And kindle it, thy holy flame bestowing.

O let it freely burn,
Till earthly passions turn
To dust and ashes in its heat consuming;
And let thy glorious light
Shine ever on my sight,
And clothe me round, the while my path illuming.

Let holy charity
Mine outward vesture be,
And lowliness become mine inner clothing;
True lowliness of heart,
Which takes the humbler part,
And o'er its own shortcomings weeps with loathing.

And so the yearning strong,
With which the soul will long,
Shall far outpass the power of human telling;
For none can guess its grace,
Till he become the place
Wherein the Holy Spirit makes his dwelling.

Bianco da Siena, d.1434;
translated by Richard Frederick Littledale

6

The Chapel of Reconciliation

The Chapel of Reconciliation, built according to the pattern of a Norfolk barn, is dark and silent within, its plain brick and warm-toned wood inviting the pilgrim to meditation and prayer.

The church was dedicated in 1982. It can accommodate a large number of people, and the wall behind the main altar can be opened out for greater gatherings which include crowds in the open air. The icon to the left of the altar was a gift from the Orthodox Church; to the right the Blessed Sacrament is reserved.

The theme of reconciliation and Christian unity is one which calls forth the longing in many hearts that Walsingham may be a centre for all Christians to unite in their love for Jesus and his mother.

Meditation

We pray to God by his holy flesh and by his precious blood, his holy Passion, his dearworthy death and his glorious wounds; but all the blessed nature and the endless life that we receive from all these are from the goodness of God. We pray to him because of the love of the sweet mother who bore him and all the help that we receive from her, but all this is the work of God's goodness.

We pray by the holy Cross on which he died, but all the help and strength that the Cross gives us comes from his goodness. In the same way, all the help that we have from special saints and all the blessed company of heaven, the inestimable love and the holy and never-ending friendship that we receive from them all, stem from God's goodness. The ways and means that God in his goodness has chosen to help us are beautiful and numerous. Of these the first and principal one is the blessed Nature which he took from the Virgin, with all the means that went before and those that are to come, which are part of our redemption and endless salvation.

Wherefore it pleases God that we seek him and worship him in these ways, knowing and recognising that he is the goodness behind everything.

To centre on the goodness of God is the highest form of prayer, and God's goodness comes to meet us at our most basic need. It gives life to our soul and makes it live and grow in grace and virtue. It is the nearest to us by nature and the readiest to bring us grace, for it is the same grace that the soul seeks and ever will, until the day in which we truly know God who has completely enfolded us all in himself.

For just as the body is clad in clothes, and the flesh in the skin, and the bones in the flesh, and the heart in the whole, so are we, body and soul, clad and enclosed in the goodness of God. Yes, and even more intimately because all these other things may wear out and vanish, but the goodness of God is always whole and close to us without compare. Truly our lover desires our soul to cling to him with all its might and to cling evermore to his goodness. For, of all the things the heart could think of, this pleases God most and soonest helps the soul to prayerfulness. Our soul is so preciously loved by him who is highest that it is far beyond the comprehension of all creatures. That is to say, no created being can fully know how much, how sweetly and how tenderly our Creator loves us. And therefore we can, with his grace and his help, remain in spiritual contemplation, endlessly marvelling at the high, surpassing, immeasurable love which our Lord in his goodness has for us. So we may reverently ask from our Lord all that we want, for our natural will is to have God, and the good will of God is to have us.

Julian of Norwich

A prayer of St Ambrose

Lord, teach me to seek you, and reveal yourself to me
     when I seek you.
For I cannot seek you unless you teach me,
nor find you except you reveal yourself.
Let me seek you in longing, let me long for you in seeking.
Let me find you in love, and love you in finding you.
     Amen.

O thou, who at thy Eucharist didst pray

O thou, who at thy Eucharist didst pray
That all thy Church might be for ever one,
Grant us at every Eucharist to say,
With longing heart and soul, 'Thy will be done.'
O may we all one bread, one body be,
One through this sacrament of unity.

For all thy Church, O Lord, we intercede;
Make thou our sad divisions soon to cease;
Draw us the nearer each to each, we plead,
By drawing all to thee, O Prince of peace;
Thus may we all one bread, one body be,
One through this sacrament of unity.

We pray thee too for wanderers from thy fold;
O bring them back, good shepherd of the sheep,
Back to the faith which saints believed of old,
Back to the Church which still that faith doth keep;
Soon may we all one bread, one body be,
One through this sacrament of unity.

So, Lord, at length when sacraments shall cease,
May we be one with all thy Church above,
One with thy saints in one unbroken peace,

One with thy saints in one unbounded love:
More blessed still, in peace and love to be
One with the Trinity in unity.

William Harry Turton;
based on John 17:11

Almighty Father

Almighty Father of our Lord, Jesus Christ,
you have revealed the beauty of your power by exalting
the lowly virgin of Nazareth
and making her the mother of our Saviour.
May the prayers of this woman bring Jesus to the waiting
world,
and fill the void of incompletion with the presence of her
Child.

Missal

Lord Jesus Christ, you said to your apostles

Lord Jesus Christ, you said to your apostles: 'I leave you
peace, my peace I give you.'
Look not on our sins, but on the faith of your Church,
and grant us the peace and unity of your kingdom where
you live for ever and ever. Amen.

Missal

7

The Anglican Shrine Church

The Anglican Shrine Church was built by Father Hope Patten in 1931 and contains a replica of the original holy house. It is a real 'people's church', many local artists and craftsmen being responsible for its decoration and adornment. Special mention must be made of the fine murals by Enid Chadwick.

The large picture that meets the eye of every pilgrim on entering the church is a copy of Andrea della Robbia's terracotta of the Annunciation in the sanctuary of La Verna, where St Francis of Assisi received the stigmata or wounds of Christ. The Annunciation is the primary mystery commemorated at Walsingham.

ᴛʜᴇ anglican Shrine Church

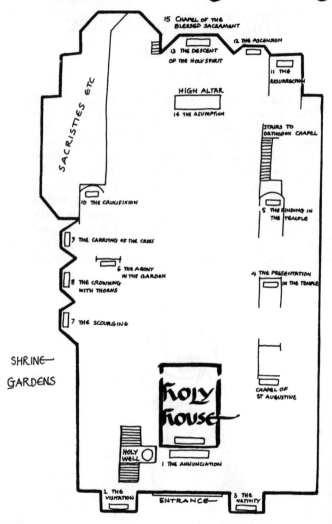

15 CHAPEL OF THE BLESSED SACRAMENT

12 THE ASCENSION

13 THE DESCENT OF THE HOLY SPIRIT

11 THE RESURRECTION

SACRISTIES ETC

HIGH ALTAR

14 THE ASUMPTION

STAIRS TO ORTHODOX CHAPEL

5 THE FINDING IN THE TEMPLE

10 THE CRUCIFIXION

9 THE CARRYING OF THE CROSS

6 THE AGONY IN THE GARDEN

4 THE PRESENTATION IN THE TEMPLE

8 THE CROWNING WITH THORNS

7 THE SCOURGING

SHRINE GARDENS

Holy House

CHAPEL OF ST AUGUSTINE

HOLY WELL

1 THE ANNUNCIATION

2 THE VISITATION

ENTRANCE

3 THE NATIVITY

The holy house which contains the statue of Our Lady of Walsingham, robed on feast days, is built of brick with inlaid pieces of stone from the sites of many abbeys and holy places in England. Within, candles burn continually as a reminder of perpetual prayer.

The Shrine Church contains many interesting statues as well as fifteen small chapels, each one dedicated to a mystery of the rosary. The last chapel, dedicated to the Crowning of Our Lady, is situated upstairs and is placed where the Sacrament is reserved for quiet prayer and private meditation. There is also a chapel for Orthodox pilgrims, although these now have their own church in Great Walsingham.

A well discovered during the Shrine's construction provides a constant supply of water for blessing and healing purposes and is a reminder to the pilgrim of his or her baptismal promises.

By the main door can be seen tablets inscribed with thanks for prayers at the Shrine which have been answered.

Meditation

Then he brought our Lady St Mary to my attention. I saw her spiritually in bodily likeness, a simple humble maiden, young in years and little more than a child, in the form in which she was when she conceived. God also showed me something of the wisdom and the truth of her soul, and through this I understood her sense of reverence with which she beheld God, her Creator. I also understood her profound wondering reverence that he, her Creator, should want to be born of her, someone so simple and of his own making. This wisdom and truth, this knowledge of her Creator's greatness and her own littleness as creature, made her say to Gabriel in deep humility: 'Behold me here, God's handmaiden!' In this vision I understood without any doubt that, as far as worthiness and wholeness are concerned, she is superior to everything else that God has made; for above her there is nothing in the created order except Jesus Christ in his humanity, as I see it.

Julian of Norwich

O Mary, give me insight

O Mary, give me insight into the true meaning of humility.
Let me realise that it means standing always in the truth,
    having nothing to hide,
acting in the light before God and before others.
Secure in the Father's love,
may I cease being afraid, deceitful, manipulative;
let my energy be devoted to surrendering totally to him
    and not protecting my own weak self.
He looks tenderly on me as he did upon you,
full of forgiveness, kindness, understanding and love.
Obtain for me, Mary, the grace to live from the certainty
    of forgiveness
and so find peace and inner healing. Amen.

Intercessions in the holy house

In the name of the Father and of the Son and of the Holy Spirit. Amen.

Father, you have shown your compassion and love by coming among us as man when your Word took flesh, born of the Virgin Mary and crucified for our salvation. As we thank you for your loving care for us, we pray that all those whom we now remember before you in this holy house may know your kindness and rejoice in your salvation. We ask this through Christ, Our Lord. Amen.

Thanksgivings may be offered. At the end a period of silence may be kept and then this prayer used:

Almighty God, Father of all mercies, we thank you for all your goodness and loving kindness to us and to all your children. Give us a sense of all your mercies, that our hearts may be grateful and our whole lives give you praise. We ask this through Christ our Lord. Amen.

For the sick

Father, your Son Jesus Christ brought healing in body and soul to those who turned to him in faith. Hear our prayers for all the sick: restore them to health and strength, comfort them with the presence of your Holy Spirit, and lead them to know and to do your will. We ask this through Christ our Lord. Amen.

For those in need

Father Almighty, have pity on all those for whom we are asked to pray in this holy place. Send them from your sanctuary the gift of your consolation and by your power and grace assist all those in spiritual and material need. Aided by the prayers of Our Lady of Walsingham we have confidence in your loving kindness, and we make these prayers through her Son, Jesus Christ our Lord. Amen.

For the departed

Lord God, you are the fountain of mercy and wish all to be saved: have mercy on all the departed whom we remember here. Through the intercession of Blessed Mary ever-virgin and of all your saints, grant that they may triumph over death and live forever before you, their Creator and Redeemer. We make our prayer through our Risen Lord Jesus Christ. Amen.

For the parish and community

Father, in Nazareth your Son shared the life of a human family and lived among your people. We remember those among whom we live, pray and work. May your Church be a sign of salvation in the world and our lives bring the presence of Christ to those around us. We ask this through

Christ your Son our Lord, who lives and reigns with you and the Holy Spirit, one God, for ever and ever. Amen.

Walsingham prayer to Our Lady

Let us ask Our Lady of Walsingham to join her prayer with those we have offered in this holy house, as we say: Hail Mary ...

O Mary, recall the solemn moment when Jesus, your divine Son, dying on the Cross, confided us to your maternal care. You are our Mother, we desire ever to remain your devout children. Let us therefore feel the effects of your powerful intercession with Jesus Christ. Make your name again glorious in this place once renowned throughout our land by your visits, favours and many miracles.

Pray, O holy Mother of God, for the conversion of England, restoration of the sick, consolation for the afflicted, repentance of sinners, peace to the departed.

O blessed Mary, Mother of God, Our Lady of Walsingham, intercede for us. Amen.

Thou who didst summon

Thou who didst summon thy servant Richeldis,
Bidding her build to thine honour a Shrine,
Help us to follow in thy blessed footsteps,
Framing our lives on the pattern divine.

Countless the pilgrims whose footsteps have echoed
Down through the years along Walsingham's Way;
Countless the prayers that thy children have offered;
Mary of Walsingham, hear us, we pray.

Many long years saw thine image neglected,
Only a few sought the help of thy prayers:
Walsingham's Shrine now again in its beauty
Welcomes each pilgrim who thither repairs.

Pray for us then, blessed Mary, our Mother,
Pray for thy children who kneel in thy Shrine,

Pray that thy Son upon England thy Dowry
Pour down his favours and blessings divine.

So shall we praise thee with ceaseless thanksgiving,
so shall we sing of thy love and thy power,
So shall we feel thy protection and comfort
All through our lives and in death's solemn hour.

8

Saint Mary's Church

Saint Mary's Church is built on the original Saxon site that Richeldis and her son Geoffrey de Favarches would have known. The present church is of later provenance, built around the fifteenth century, but the inside was gutted by fire in 1961. Fortunately the Seven Sacrament font, together with much fine brass and stone carving, was preserved. There is a magnificent east window telling the story of Walsingham, and the remodelled interior is full of light, giving a sense of spaciousness and joy.

In the Guild's chapel to the left of the sanctuary, where Father Hope Patten first set up a statue of Our Lady of Walsingham (the one now in the holy house), there is a small replica in memory of earlier times. Mary looks out towards the priory grounds, her Child on her lap. Here devotion to Our Lady of Walsingham in the Anglican Church originated and continues to the present day.

Prayer to Our Lady of Walsingham

O alone of all women, Mother and Virgin,
Mother most happy, Virgin most pure.
We, impure as we are, come to you who are all pure.
We greet you, we praise you how we may with our
    humble self-offering.
May your Son grant us that, imitating your holy surrender,
we too, by the grace of the Holy Spirit, may deserve to
    conceive the Lord Jesus in our inmost soul,
and once conceived, never to lose him. Amen.

Erasmus

The Litany of Our Lady (or the Litany of Loreto)

Lord, have mercy. *Lord, have mercy.*
Christ, have mercy. *Christ, have mercy.*
Lord, have mercy. *Lord, have mercy.*
Christ, hear us. *Christ, graciously hear us*

God the Father of heaven, *have mercy on us.*
God the Son, redeemer of the world, *have mercy on us.*
God the Holy Spirit, *have mercy on us.*
Holy Trinity, one God, *have mercy on us.*

Holy Mary, *pray for us.*
Holy Mother of God, *pray for us.*
Holy Virgin of virgins, *pray for us.*
Mother of Christ, *pray for us.*
Mother of divine grace, *pray for us.*
Mother most pure, *pray for us.*
Mother most chaste, *pray for us.*
Mother inviolate, *pray for us.*
Mother undefiled, *pray for us.*
Mother most lovable, *pray for us.*
Mother most admirable, *pray for us.*
Mother of good counsel, *pray for us.*
Mother of our creator, *pray for us.*
Mother of our Saviour, *pray for us.*
Virgin most prudent, *pray for us.*
Virgin most venerable, *pray for us.*

Virgin most renowned, *pray for us.*
Virgin most powerful, *pray for us.*
Virgin most merciful, *pray for us.*
Virgin most faithful, *pray for us.*
Mirror of justice, *pray for us.*
Seat of wisdom, *pray for us.*
Cause of our joy, *pray for us.*
Spiritual vessel, *pray for us.*
Vessel of honour, *pray for us.*
Singular vessel of devotion, *pray for us.*
Mystical rose, *pray for us.*
Tower of David, *pray for us.*
Tower of ivory, *pray for us.*
House of gold, *pray for us.*
Arc of the covenant, *pray for us.*
Gate of heaven, *pray for us.*
Morning star, *pray for us.*
Health of the sick, *pray for us.*
Refuge of sinners, *pray for us.*
Comfort of the afflicted, *pray for us.*
Help of Christians, *pray for us.*
Queen of angels, *pray for us.*
Queen of patriarchs, *pray for us.*
Queen of prophets, *pray for us.*
Queen of apostles, *pray for us.*
Queen of martyrs, *pray for us.*
Queen of confessors, *pray for us.*
Queen of virgins, *pray for us.*
Queen of all saints, *pray for us.*
Queen conceived without original sin, *pray for us.*
Queen assumed into heaven, *pray for us.*
Queen of the most holy rosary, *pray for us.*
Queen of peace, *pray for us.*

Lamb of God, you take away the sins of the world, *spare us, O Lord.*
Lamb of God, you take away the sins of the world, *graciously hear us, O Lord.*
Lamb of God, you take away the sins of the world, *have mercy on us.*

Pray for us, O holy Mother of God, *that we may be*
worthy of the promises of Christ.

Let us pray

Grant that we your servants, Lord, may enjoy unfailing
health of mind and body, and through the prayers of the
ever Blessed Virgin Mary in her glory, free us from our
sorrows in this world and give us eternal happiness in the
next. Through Christ our Lord. Amen.

The heavens are mine

The heavens are mine, the earth is mine, and the nations
are mine. Mine are the just and mine are the sinners. The
angels are mine and the Mother of God, and all things are
mine. God himself is mine and for me, because Christ is
mine and all for me. What then do you seek, what do you
ask for then my soul? Everything is yours and for you.
Rejoice then, and you shall receive all the desires of your
heart.

St John of the Cross

As the bridegroom to his chosen

As the bridegroom to his chosen,
As the king unto his realm,
As the keep unto the castle,
As the pilot to the helm,
So, Lord, art Thou to me.

As the fountain to the garden,
As the candle in the dark,
As the treasure in the coffer,
As the manna in the ark,
So, Lord, art Thou to me.

As the ruby in the setting,
As the honey in the comb,
As the light within the lantern,

As the Father in the home,
So, Lord, art Thou to me.

As the sunshine in the heavens,
As the image in the glass,
As the fruit unto the fig-tree,
As the dew unto the grass,
So, Lord, are Thou to me.

Blessed Henry Suso

9

The Priory or 'The Abbey'

The site of the former Augustinian priory, now known as 'the Abbey', is in private hands, but on most days of the year it is open to visitors and pilgrims at stated times. Nearly all the big pilgrimages include services in these grounds, where once a large priory church stood and where the original holy house witnessed a constant stream of pilgrims to Our Lady.

The site of Richeldis' first holy house is marked, and there are parts of the priory buildings extant, the most notable being the solitary arch of the east window, stark against the sky. Behind the arch can be seen the holy wells and the stone bath, presumably used for immersing the sick under the patronage of St Lawrence.

The priory was founded in 1153 and housed a community of Augustinian Canons who cared for pilgrims. They built a magnificent church within which the holy house was enshrined.

After the Dissolution of the Monasteries by Henry VIII the buildings fell into ruin because, unlike many other abbey and priory churches which subsequently were used for parish worship, Walsingham had its own separate parish church.

The ruins of the Franciscan friary, on another site, are the best preserved Franciscan ruins in England. They are seldom accessible to the public, although they can be seen quite clearly from the road.

Psalm 84

How lovely is your dwelling place,
Lord, God of hosts.

My soul is longing and yearning,
is yearning for the courts of the Lord.
My heart and my soul ring out their joy
to God, the living God.

The sparrow herself finds a home
and the swallow a nest for her brood;
she lays her young by your altars,
Lord of hosts, my king and my God.

They are happy who dwell in your house,
for ever singing your praise.
They are happy whose strength is in you,
in whose hearts are the roads to Sion.

As they go through the Bitter Valley
they make it a place of springs,
the autumn rain covers it with blessings.
They walk with ever growing strength,
they will see the God of gods in Sion.

O Lord God of hosts, hear my prayer,
give ear, O God of Jacob.
Turn your eyes O God our shield,
look on the face of your anointed.

One day within your courts
is better than a thousand elsewhere.
The threshold of the house of God
I prefer to the dwellings of the wicked.

For the Lord God is a rampart, a shield;
he will give us his favour and glory.
The Lord will not refuse any good
to those who walk without blame.

Lord, God of hosts,
happy the one who trusts in you!

O sweetest love of God

O sweetest love of God too little known, whoever finds you
is at rest; let everything change, O my God, that we may
rest in you. O my God, how sweet your presence is to me,
you who are the one true Good. I will rejoice in nothing
until I am in your arms. O Lord, I beseech you, leave me
not for a moment, because I know not the value of my soul.
Amen.

St John of the Cross

Long ago in Nazareth

Long ago in Nazareth dwelt a Virgin fair,
Spring was in her heart and spring was in the air.
All underground the seeds were sprouting green,
Love would bloom with them though now they were
    unseen.

'Hail O Holy Mary,' spoke an angel voice,
'For the Lord is with you, sing aloud, rejoice!
Laid in dark earth, to mortal eyes unseen
Love will come to you like wheat that springeth green.'

'I am the Lord's servant,' answered she with grace,
And the joy of springtime shone upon her face.
Love in her womb, would blossom where had been
Nothing but the soil for wheat springeth green.

So the darkened world will radiant be with light,
For an angel's message pierces through life's night.
Love now will live where death and sin have been,
Mary shall bring forth the wheat that springeth green.

Joyfully to Mary Virgin let us sing,
All for she gave us Jesus Christ our King.
Love did she bear, of love is she the Queen,
Love has come to us, like wheat that springeth green.

O Mary, you are the 'good ground'

O Mary, you are the 'good ground' on which the seed fell.
You have brought forth fruit a hundredfold. Draw us close
to your loving heart and keep us there in gentle lowliness
and perfect trust. Teach us to receive the Spirit as you did;
to open our hearts to the Sacred Word, to ponder it in
silence and yield a rich harvest. Teach us to be apostles of
love.

Ruth Burrows

Saint Teresa's bookmark

Let nothing disturb you,
Let nothing affright you,
All things pass away;
God alone abideth.
Patience obtains all things;
Whoever has God
Can want for nothing,
God alone sufficeth.

St Teresa of Avila

Canticle of the creatures

All highest, omnipotent, good Lord, to you be praise, glory
and honour and every blessing.
To you alone they are due, and no one is worthy to speak
your name.
Be praised my Lord for all creatures, especially Brother
Sun, who makes daytime,

and through him you give us light. He is beautiful, radiant
with great splendour,
and he is a sign that tells, All-Highest, of you.
Be praised my Lord for Sister Moon and the stars,
You formed them in the sky, bright and precious and
beautiful.
Be praised my Lord for Brother Wind, and for the air and
the clouds,
and for fair and every kind of weather by which you give
your creatures food.
Be praised my Lord for Sister Water, who is most humble
and useful, lovely and chaste.
Be praised my Lord for Brother Fire, through whom you
light up the night for us,
and he is beautiful and jolly, lusty and strong.
Be praised my Lord for our sister, Mother Earth, who keeps
us and feeds us,
and brings forth fruits of many kinds, with coloured
flowers and plants as well.
Be praised my Lord for those who grant pardon for love of
you and bear with sickness and vexation.
Blessed are those who bear these things peaceably
because by you, All-Highest, they will be crowned.
Be praised my Lord for our sister Death, whom no living
person can escape.
Woe to those who die in mortal sin. Blessed are those
whom she will find doing your holy will,
For to them the second death will do no harm.
Bless and praise my Lord, thank him and serve him in all
humility.

St Francis of Assisi

10

The Rosary of Our Lady

The rosary is a very old prayer by which we contemplate the life of Jesus through the eyes of his mother; for this we use special beads, and as the beads pass through our fingers we spend time thinking on the mystery before us. There are five joyful mysteries: the Annunciation, the Visitation, the Nativity, the Presentation in the temple and the Finding of Jesus in the temple. The five sorrowful mysteries are: the Agony in the Garden, the Scourging, the Crowning with thorns, the Carrying of the Cross and the Crucifixion of Jesus. The five glorious mysteries are: the Resurrection, the Ascension, the Descent of the Holy Spirit at Pentecost, the Assumption of our Blessed Lady and her Crowning in heaven.

The Rosary is made up of 'decades'. A decade is one 'Our Father' followed by ten 'Hail Marys' and a 'Glory be'. It is usual to say five decades at a time, either the joyful, sorrowful or glorious mysteries.

Begin with the sign on the cross. Pray the Apostles' Creed holding the crucifix and continue on the straight piece of the rosary with one 'Our Father', three 'Hail Marys' and a 'Glory be'. Then to start the first decade pray one 'Our Father', continue with ten 'Hail Marys', and end with a 'Glory be'. Each decade gives you time to think on one of the mysteries as you pray the 'Hail Marys'. When you have completed five decades, end with the 'Hail, Holy Queen' and any other prayers you may wish to add.

Hail, holy queen

Hail, holy queen, Mother of mercy; hail, our life, our sweetness, and our hope; to thee do we cry, poor banished children of Eve; to thee do we send up our sighs, mourning and weeping in this valley of tears. Turn then, most gracious advocate, thine eyes of mercy towards us; and after this our exile, show unto us the blessed fruit of thy womb, Jesus, O clement, O loving, O sweet Virgin Mary.

V. Queen of the most holy rosary, pray for us.
R. That we may be made worthy of the promises of Christ.

Let us pray

O God, whose only-begotten Son, by his life, death and resurrection has purchased for us the rewards of eternal life; grant, we beseech you, that meditating upon these mysteries in the most holy rosary of the Blessed Virgin Mary, we may both imitate what they contain and obtain what they promise, through the same Christ our Lord. Amen.

The joyful mysteries

1. The Annunciation

Consider how Mary says 'Yes' to conceiving Jesus in her womb. Ask for the grace to say your own 'Yes' to bringing Jesus into the world through your own life.

2. The visitation

Consider Mary visiting her cousin Elizabeth and the joy the two women share in praising God for all his mercies. Ask for the grace to take Jesus with you to all the people you meet this day, and for a spirit of gratitude and joy.

3. The nativity

Consider the scene in the stable on that first Christmas: Mary with the Child wrapped in swaddling clothes, Joseph watching over them with love and care, the shepherds coming when they hear the angel's message. Ask for the grace to welcome Jesus, however he wants to come to you.

4. The presentation in the temple

Consider Mary and Joseph taking the Child Jesus to the temple to offer him to the Father, and Simeon's prophecy that a sword would pierce Mary's heart. Ask for the grace to bear suffering willingly for Jesus' sake and for parents to love their children even when they are a cause of pain.

5. The finding of the Child Jesus in the temple

Consider Jesus at twelve years old when his parents search for him in Jerusalem at Passover time and find him after three days. Ask for the grace to be sensitive to the needs of growing children as they find their independence, and for perseverance in seeking Jesus in your own life.

The sorrowful mysteries

1. The agony in the garden

Consider Jesus in the Garden of Olives, praying that his Father will spare him the Passion if it is possible. His disciples sleep, and so Jesus faces his agony alone as he accepts the Father's will and goes forward to suffer on our behalf. Ask for the grace to seek and accept God's will even when it is costly.

2. The scourging at the pillar

Consider Jesus cruelly whipped by men who show no mercy. He has consented to undergo his Passion out of love for us and to bear pain patiently. Ask for the grace to suffer sickness or pain when it comes, and pray for all who at this moment are undergoing torture or are in any way helpless before their tormentors.

3. The crowning with thorns

Consider Jesus mocked as a king, his head running with blood, exposed to crowds who clamour for his death. Ask for the grace to think well of others even when they cause us suffering, and pray for all who are mocked because of some disability or handicap.

4. The carrying of the Cross

Consider Jesus weighed down under the Cross as he bears it to Calvary. Ask for the grace to carry your own cross in union with him, and in a spirit of solidarity with all who are suffering in mind or body.

5. The crucifixion

Consider Jesus dying in agony on behalf of the human race, showing us what it really means to continue loving and forgiving to the last. Ask for the grace to love and forgive others as Jesus has done; and pray for all who will die today, for the grace of a happy death for them, and for yourself when the time comes.

The glorious mysteries

1. The Resurrection

Consider Jesus rising in glory on Easter morning and the joy of his mother and the disciples as they realise that he has conquered death forever. Ask for the grace of a deep faith in the risen Lord, and pray for those who mourn the loss of a loved one, that they may be comforted.

2. The Ascension

Consider Mary and the disciples seeing Jesus ascend to his Father and knowing that they will see him no more on earth. Ask for the grace to believe in the continued presence of Jesus with us through his Church, and pray for those who seek him in hidden ways, finding it difficult to believe he is with them in darkness.

3. The descent of the Holy Spirit

Consider Mary and the disciples receiving the Holy Spirit while at prayer in Jerusalem. Ask for the grace to be filled with the Spirit of courage and joy to proclaim Jesus to the world, and pray that others may recognize his presence in your life and in the lives of all Christians.

4. The Assumption

Consider the happiness of Mary as, after her death, she joins her Son, body and soul in the glory of heaven. Ask for the grace to reverence your own body and the bodies of others, destined as we all are for glory, and pray for those who abuse or are abused by others, that they may realise that our bodies are the temples of the Holy Spirit.

5. The coronation of Our Lady in Heaven

Consider Mary received by Jesus into his presence and rewarded for her life of faithfulness. Ask for the grace of final perseverance, and pray for all friends, family and dear ones, that we may all meet one day in heaven and praise God forever.

11

The Stations of the Cross

In making the Stations of the Cross we walk in spirit with Jesus to Calvary, remembering all that he has suffered on our behalf. At the same time we pray for all who, at this moment, are sharing in some way in the redemption of the world through their own suffering. One day with Jesus, we and they will know the joy of resurrection if we persevere to the end.

There are outdoor Stations of the Cross in the grounds of both shrines as well as in the churches.

Opening prayer

Jesus, I am about to make the Way of the Cross. Be with me, and help me to understand the love with which you suffered; a love you want to share with me now as I walk with you to Calvary. Amen.

1. Jesus is condemned to death

Jesus stands before Pilate bound and humiliated. A robber has been preferred before him because the leaders are jealous of Jesus' freedom and goodness. His way of living has shown them up for the mean-spirited people they are.

For his part, Pilate has been cowardly in condemning a man he knows to be innocent. He is more interested in saving his own skin than in saving Jesus, a helpless prisoner.

It isn't always easy to take responsibility for my decisions and choices, and act according to my conscience. It may mean going against the crowd and that takes courage. Or I can judge and condemn others because they touch something in me that I don't want to look at: my jealousy, my fear, my desire for respectability at all costs.

Prayer: *Jesus, help me to stand with you in truth and be ready to take the consequences of being a person of integrity. Amen.*

2. Jesus accepts the Cross

Jesus takes the Cross that is laid upon him. It isn't something he has chosen. It is something given; something he would no doubt have rather been without, but for our sake he accepts it with love.

Life brings its crosses to each of us. I do not choose my suffering, rather it is chosen for me, given to me. What makes a difference is how I accept it. If I do so grudgingly, if I grumble and complain, I only make things worse.

But if, like Jesus, I accept with love the painful and difficult things of life as being laid on me by a loving Father, then I shall discover that these will take me, not just to Calvary, but to the joy of the Resurrection.

Prayer: *Jesus, help me to put as much love as possible into bearing the difficulties of life. May I shoulder my cross with you beside me. With you may I understand that love makes all burdens light. Amen.*

3. Jesus falls the first time

Jesus does not march off to Calvary like some strong superman. He goes as one who is weak, one who stumbles and falls. What a consolation for us when we see that Jesus is fully human! He has to get up and go on even though the way is painful, even though he finds himself down in the dust.

I often fall; but then I am tempted to stay down and complain, or say it's no use trying any more.

I don't like to look foolish, someone who doesn't succeed at first go. But neither did Jesus.

The only difference is that I don't get up and go on as he did, relying on the Father to give me strength.

Prayer: *Jesus, never let me give up, no matter how often I fall. Keep my eyes on the goal and help me to go forward with you beside me. Amen.*

4. Jesus meets his mother

It must have been terribly hard for Jesus to know that he was causing his mother so much suffering. It's easier to bear pain ourselves than to see those we love suffer.
But Jesus and Mary both understand that this is part of God's plan for them and for the world.

So many mothers, members of families and close friends are in anguish in many places even today, because they are separated from those they love by war, prison, persecution or exile.

Mary can be for them, and for us, the model of someone who selflessly allows a loved one to embrace their own destiny, and offers silent, strong support without any self-pity.

Prayer: *Jesus and Mary, show me how to bear suffering with and for others, not thinking of myself but of them. Amen.*

5. Jesus is helped by Simon of Cyrene

Scripture tells of how a passer-by, Simon of Cyrene, was forced to help Jesus carry the Cross. Jesus was so weak from sleeplessness and loss of blood that his captors were afraid he would not reach Calvary alive.

No doubt Simon felt put upon. It was Passover time and he was on holiday, yet he had to shoulder the cross of a condemned criminal. Only later he must have realised that this was not his moment of shame but his moment of glory, the only incident in his life which would make him remembered.

Do I help others who suffer, or am I too busy

grumbling about my own lot in life? If I do help, it is truly Jesus himself whom I relieve of his burden.

Prayer: *Jesus, help me to recognise you in those who suffer, and be always ready to lend a hand cheerfully. Amen.*

6. Veronica wipes the face of Jesus

It is only legend which says that a woman came forward to wipe the face of Jesus as he stumbled on, and then found his face impressed on the linen she had used. Tradition then gave her the name of Veronica – that is, *vera icon* or 'true image'.

Many people are mocked, taunted or despised because of their race, colour or religion. In many cases we avoid those who are different from ourselves. We don't want to get involved, like the crowd who just stood and watched Jesus go to Calvary. Only one person had the courage to do an act of kindness on her own initiative.

Am I like Veronica when it comes to showing sympathy for those who are marginalized? If so, then Jesus will imprint his image on my own heart.

Prayer: *Jesus, you said that what is done to the least person is done to you. Give me the courage to reach out and help all who need it. Then I too will become a bearer of your image on earth. Amen.*

7. Jesus falls a second time

Another fall. What a humiliation! Jesus finds himself down in the mud and dust once again. He certainly doesn't look clean and heroic; he is weary, dirty, jeered at by the onlookers.

Even though Simon has relieved Jesus of some of the weight, he is still unable to cope.

How hard it can be for me to accept my weaknesses patiently when it seems that others are laughing at my failures.

Jesus can show me how to turn my falls into steps that take me on to victory if only I continue in his company, relying not on myself but on him, who knows what it is to be seen as a failure.

Prayer: *Jesus, show me how to make the most of my falls by learning from them to rely on your grace and not on my own strength. Amen.*

8. The women of Jerusalem mourn for Jesus

The women of Jerusalem wept when they saw Jesus going to crucifixion. They may have been professional mourners hired to accompany condemned criminals to execution, or they may just have been women who felt a natural sympathy for Jesus, who had always treated women with respect.

But Jesus tells them that their tears are wasted on him. It is they and their children who will suffer more when, in the future, Jerusalem will be put to the sword.

It isn't easy to see clearly enough to weep for the right things. I can weep uselessly for Jesus who died long ago, and yet I don't see that I am asked instead to comfort a bereaved neighbour, a refugee who is a stranger in my town, an elderly person who longs for a visit.

Prayer: *Jesus, help me to see where sympathy is really needed and offer it willingly. Amen.*

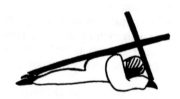

9. Jesus falls a third time

Another fall. Jesus is utterly exhausted as he approaches Calvary. He wonders if he will ever get there alive. Yet he knows he must, and so he forces himself to continue.

It's like trying to cope with a fault of my own such as impatience, meanness, bad temper. I fall, I fall again ... and again ... I make up my mind that I won't fall again; but I do, countless times. No remedy seems to work!

But that is the moment when I can rely on Jesus to help me not to give up in despair. He knows what it is to be weak and needy. He knows too that in the end there is victory if I persevere. Trying, not succeeding, makes the difference.

Prayer: *Jesus, however hard my own path seems, may I trust you to see me through to the end. Amen.*

10. Jesus is stripped of his garments

Jesus is shamed by being stripped in front of everyone before being nailed to the Cross.

Clothes give us a sense of dignity, but nakedness is considered shameful. That is why unjust regimes often strip prisoners before interrogation and torture. It makes them feel exposed and vulnerable.

On the other hand, sick people have to be helped by others to perform the most private bodily functions.

Jesus accepts being naked because he has absolutely nothing to hide. His dignity doesn't consist in fine clothes or being nicely dressed. It consists in his status as a child of God, who is loved just as he is, without any disguise.

Prayer: *Jesus, help me to give others a proper respect at all times rather than judging by outward appearances. Amen.*

11. Jesus is nailed to the Cross

Jesus must have experienced terrible agony when the nails were driven through his flesh, pinning his body to the Cross. No longer could he move by himself; he had only to wait now for death to come as he hung helpless and in pain.

I too am nailed to the cross of my life by things I cannot help or change: illness, temperamental difficulties, lack of talent, traumas suffered in childhood which have left a permanent mark, personal sin.

Or maybe I have chosen a way of life that deprives me of personal freedom because I must serve and help others. I am nailed by circumstances and cannot move. Whatever the case, I can be sure that Jesus is with me and with all who suffer.

Prayer: *Jesus, you were nailed to the Cross and held there by love. May I love what holds me on my cross with you. Amen.*

12. Jesus dies on the Cross

We all have to die at some time, but Jesus dies when he is still young. He dies unjustly, by violence. Yet he forgives those who have tormented him and condemned him. He promises paradise to the robber crucified with him. He remembers his mother who stands by the Cross, and confides her to the care of the apostle John. Jesus doesn't leave any loose ends behind him, so he is able to say at the last, 'All is finished. Father, I place my soul in your loving hands.'

Let us pray for all who are dying today, especially those who die young, those who die suddenly through war or violence, those who die unloved or uncared for.

And may I too be ready for my own death when it comes.

Prayer: *Holy Mary, Mother of God, pray for us sinners now and at the hour of our death Amen.*

13. Jesus is taken down from the Cross

When he is dead, Jesus is taken down from the Cross and laid in his mother's arms. Can we even imagine what it must have been like for Mary to hold her dead son after seeing him die in agony?

But Mary understands, even in her sorrow, that Jesus has accomplished the Father's will, so beneath her tears she is at peace.

It isn't easy to accept that loved ones must die.

It isn't easy to see why or to what purpose they have been taken from us. All we can do is believe in faith that 'All shall be well, and all shall be well, and all manner of things shall be well' (Julian of Norwich).

We cannot see into God's designs. All we know is that he never deserts anyone, no matter what.

Prayer: *Father, help me to trust even in sorrow, believing that you have a plan for each one, just as you had a plan for your own Son. Amen.*

14. Jesus is laid in the tomb

All is silent now. Jesus is buried as his friends mourn. The stone is rolled in front of the tomb. It seems as if everything is over for ever. A beautiful and compassionate person has been killed, his life ended.

Death always seems so final.

But we know that this is not really the end. God the Father will raise Jesus to life because his was a life of total love – and love endures for ever.

What seems like failure is really victory. Jesus has conquered death for ever.

Right now Jesus is silent, dead, buried; but inwardly life and love are ready to burst forth eternally.

Can I too trust that, in all the little deaths of my life, God is awaiting the moment to bring forth something new and better, if only I give him time?

Prayer: *Lord, I believe. Help my unbelief. Amen.*

15. The Resurrection

Jesus is risen. Alleluia!
  Jesus is alive. Alleluia!
  Jesus brings joy.
  Jesus brings peace.
  He asks us not to be afraid, to touch his wounds
and know that he now lives for ever.
  In him we too have life, peace, joy. These are his
gifts to us. We have only to ask for them.

Prayer: *Lord Jesus Christ, by your saving death and resurrection free me from every sin and all evil. May your peace take root in my heart and bring forth a harvest of love, holiness, joy and truth. Amen.*

12

Vespers of Our Lady of Walsingham

V. O God, come to our aid.
R. O Lord, make haste to help us. Glory be ...

Hymn

The angel Gabriel from heaven came,
his wings as drifted snow, his eyes as flame.
'All hail,' said he, 'thou lowly maiden Mary,
most highly favoured lady.' *Gloria.*

'For now a blessed mother thou shalt be,
all generations laud and honour thee.
Thy Son shall be Emmanuel, by seers foretold,
most highly favoured lady.' *Gloria.*

Then gentle Mary meekly bowed her head,
'To me be as it pleases God,' she said.
'My soul shall laud and magnify his holy name.'
Most highly favoured lady. *Gloria.*

Antiphon

Do not be afraid, Mary, for you have found favour with God. Behold, you will conceive and bear a son, and he will be called the Son of the Most High.

Psalm 121

I rejoiced when I heard them say,
'Let us go to God's house.'
And now our feet are standing
within your gates, O Jerusalem.

Jerusalem is built as a city
strongly compact.
It is there that the tribes go up,
the tribes of the Lord.

For Israel's law it is
there to praise the Lord's name.
There were set the thrones of judgement
of the house of David.

For the peace of Jerusalem pray:
'Peace be to your homes!
May peace reign in your walls,
in your palaces, peace!'

For love of my brethren and friends
I say: 'Peace upon you!'
For love of the house of the Lord
I will ask for your good.
Glory be ...

Antiphon

Do not be afraid, Mary, for you have found favour with God. Behold, you will conceive and bear a son, and he will be called the Son of the Most High.

Antiphon

I am the servant of the Lord; let it be as you have said.

Psalm 131

O Lord, my heart is not proud,
nor haughty my eyes.
I have not gone after things too great,
nor marvels beyond me.

Truly I have set my soul
in silence and peace;
as a child has rest in its mother's arms,
even so is my soul.

O Israel, hope in the Lord,
both now and for ever.
Glory be ...

Antiphon

I am the servant of the Lord; let it be as you have said.

Antiphon

The Word of God, born of the Father before time began,
humbled himself for love of us, and became man.

Philippians 2:6–11

Though he was in the form of God,
Jesus did not count equality with God a thing to be
        grasped.

He emptied himself, taking the form of a servant,
being born in human likeness.

And being found in human form,
he humbled himself and became obedient unto death,
even death on a cross.

Therefore God has highly exalted him,
and bestowed on him the name which is above every
     name,

that at the name of Jesus every knee should bow,
in heaven and on earth and under the earth,

and every tongue confess that Jesus Christ is Lord,
to the glory of God the Father.
Glory be ...

Antiphon

The Word of God, born of the Father before time began,
humbled himself for love of us, and became man.

Scripture

Sing aloud, O daughter of Sion, shout O Israel!
Rejoice and exult with all your heart, O daughter of
     Jerusalem!
The King of Israel, the Lord, is in your midst; you shall fear
     evil no more.
He will rejoice over you with gladness, he will renew you
     in his love.

Responsary

Hail Mary, full of grace, the Lord is with you.
*Response (R): Hail Mary, full of grace, the Lord is with
     you.*
Blessed are you among women, and blest the fruit of your
     womb. *R.*
Glory be to the Father and to the Son and to the Holy
     Spirit. *R.*

Magnificat

(Tune: 'Amazing Grace')

My soul proclaims the Lord my God,
my spirit sings his praise.
He looks on me, he lifts me up,
and gladness fills my days.

All nations now will share my joy;
his gifts he has outpoured.
His little ones he has made great;
I magnify the Lord.

His mercy is forevermore;
his holy name I praise.
His strong right arm puts down the proud;
the lowly he does raise.

He fills the hungry with good things;
the rich he sends away.
The promise made to Abraham
is fulfilled by him each day.

To Father, Son and Spirit blessed,
the God whom we adore,
be glory, as it was, is now,
and shall be evermore.

Intercessions

The response (R.) is: *'Lord, fill us with your grace.'*

Eternal Father, through your angel you made known your
salvation to Mary. Full of confidence, we earnestly pray. *R.*

By the consent of your handmaid and the power of the
Holy Spirit, your Word came to dwell among us. Open our
hearts to receive Christ as Mary the Virgin received him. *R.*

You look with compassion on the lowly and fill the starving with good things. Encourage the downhearted, help all those in need and comfort those near to death. *R.*

You called Mary to be mother in the house of Jesus and Joseph. Through her prayers help all mothers to make their homes places of love and holiness. *R.*

Mary was your faithful handmaid who treasured your words in her heart. Through her intercession let us become devoted disciples of Jesus your Son. *R.*

Let the dead enter with joy into your presence, to rejoice with Mary and all the saints before you. *R.*

Let us join our prayers with Mary as we pray in the words which her Son gave us: *Our Father ...*

Let us pray

Lord, open our hearts to your grace.
Through the angel's message to Mary
we have learned to believe in the Incarnation of Christ
     your Son;
lead us by his Passion and Cross to the glory of his
     Resurrection.
We make our prayer through our Lord Jesus Christ your
     Son,
who lives and reigns with you in the unity of the Holy
     Spirit,
one God for ever and ever. Amen.

13

The Sacrament of Reconciliation

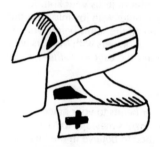

In the Sacrament of Reconciliation we proclaim our sinfulness before God and celebrate the joy of forgiveness. This Sacrament should be a source of great peace and happiness for us, because our faith assures us of the forgiveness of sins through the Passion, Death and Resurrection of Jesus Christ our Lord.

Before going into the confessional or the reconciliation room, spend time quietly pondering, reflecting on your life. Ask the Lord to show you where you fail most and what you have done wrong. Realise that you are bringing yourself before a loving and forgiving God who is waiting to receive you and welcome you home.

Some of the following biblical passages may help you to prepare your mind and heart:

'Wash me from my guilt and cleanse me from my sin'.

Ps. 51

'Though your sins are like scarlet they shall be white as
   snow'.   *Isa. 1:16–18*
'I will heal their faithlessness and love them freely'.
                                                          Hosea 14:4–7
'Have courage, your sins are forgiven,' Jesus says to the
   paralytic.   *Matt. 9:1–8*
Jesus eats with tax collectors and sinners. He has not
   come to call the righteous but sinners.   *Matt. 9:9–13*
Jesus calls to himself all who are weighed down by heavy
   burdens.   *Matt. 11:25–30*
The sinful woman anoints Jesus. All her sins are forgiven
   because she has loved so much.   *Luke 7:36–50*
Jesus goes after the lost sheep and rejoices when he finds
   it.   *Luke 15:1–7*
The father welcomes home the prodigal son and prepares
   a feast for him.   *Luke 15:11–32*
Jesus forgives even the men who are crucifying him.
                                                          Luke 23:32–34
Jesus gives his apostles power to forgive sins and to
   proclaim his peace.   *John 20:19–23*

When you go in to the priest, kneel or sit as you wish.
The priest will say a few words of welcome or read a
short passage from the Bible. Then tell your sins in a
simple and straightforward way, mentioning especially any serious wrongs you may have done. After
you have finished the priest may give you some
encouragement or advice and tell you to say some
prayers as a form of penance. Then he will invite you
to make an act of sorrow. You can do this in your own
words or in the words of one of the following prayers:

Lord Jesus Christ, you chose to be called the friend of
sinners. By your saving Death and Resurrection free me
from my sins and from every evil. May your peace take root
in my heart and bring forth a harvest of love, holiness and
truth. Amen.

Heavenly Father, Jesus told us how lovingly you welcome home the sinful child who returns to you. I come before you with sorrow. Purify my heart and give me the grace to live the new life of Easter, ever confident in your saving power. Amen.

Lord Jesus, you are the Lamb of God who takes away the sins of the world. Cleanse my soul of all sin, renew in me the grace of my Baptism and help me to live in peace with all. Amen.

Lord Jesus Christ, look not on my sins but on the faith of your Church. Create a clean heart within me, and in your goodness lead me along the path of light. Amen.

Heavenly Father, I believe in your mercy and forgiveness. Heal my soul, for I have sinned against you. I ask this through Christ our Lord. Amen.

After you have made an act of sorrow the priest will pronounce over you the forgiveness of God in these words:

God the Father of mercies,
through the Death and Resurrection of his Son,
has reconciled the world to himself
and sent the Holy Spirit among us for the forgiveness of
    sins.
Through the ministry of the Church
may God give you pardon and peace,
and I absolve you from your sins
✝ in the name of the Father, and of the Son, and of the Holy
    Spirit. Amen.
The Lord has freed you from your sins. Go in the peace of
    Christ. Amen.

When you leave the confessional kneel down and say your penance. Then spend some time in quiet prayer, praising God for his goodness in giving us this wonderful Sacrament.

Meditation

The same true love that touches us all with blessed comfort, the very same blessed love teaches us to hate sin for love's sake alone. And I am certain from my own experience that the more each loving soul sees this in the courteous love of our Lord God, the greater will be its reluctance to sin, and the more will it be ashamed.

When we have fallen through frailty or blindness, then our courteous Lord raises us up with his gentle touch and protects us. He wants us to see how wretched we are and humbly face up to it. But he does not want us to stay like that, or to be preoccupied with self-accusation or to wallow in self-pity. He wants us quickly to attend to him, for he stands all alone, and he is always waiting for us, sorrowing and grieving until we come. He hurries to bring us back to himself, for we are his joy and his delight, and he is our salvation and our life.

Julian of Norwich

14

Prayers for Before and After Holy Communion

Psalm 22

The Lord is my shepherd;
there is nothing I shall want.
Fresh and green are the pastures
where he gives me repose.
Near restful waters he leads me,
to revive my drooping spirit.

He guides me along the right path;
he is true to his name.
If I should walk in the valley of darkness
no evil would I fear.
You are there with your crook and your staff;
with these you give me comfort.

You have prepared a banquet for me
in the sight of my foes.
My head you have anointed with oil;
my cup is overflowing.

Surely goodness and kindness shall follow me
all the days of my life.
In the Lord's own house shall I dwell
for ever and ever.

O Life, giving life to all!

O Life, giving life to all! Do not deny me that living water
which you promised to all who longed for it. I thirst for it,
Lord, I long for it, I come to you.

St Teresa of Avila

God, of your goodness

God, of your goodness give me yourself, for you are
    enough for me.
I cannot ask anything less to be worthy of you.
If I were to ask less I should always be in want.
Only in you have I all.

Julian of Norwich

Almighty and ever living God

Almighty and ever living God,
I approach the sacrament of your only-begotten Son,
our Lord Jesus Christ.
I come sick to the doctor of life,
unclean to the fountain of mercy,
blind to the radiance of eternal light,
and poor and needy to the Lord of heaven and earth.
Lord, in your great generosity,
heal my sickness, wash away my defilement,
enlighten my blindness, enrich my poverty,
and clothe my nakedness.
May I receive the bread of angels,
the King of kings and Lord of lords,
with humble reverence,
with purity and faith,
with repentance and love, and the determined purpose
that will help to bring me to salvation.
May I receive the sacrament of the Lord's body and blood,
and its reality and power.
Kind God,
may I receive the body of your only-begotten Son,
our Lord Jesus Christ,
born from the womb of the Virgin Mary,

and so be received into his mystical body,
and numbered among his members.
Loving Father,
as on my earthly pilgrimage
I now receive your beloved Son
under the veil of a sacrament,
may I one day see him face to face in glory,
who lives and reigns with you for ever. Amen.

St Thomas Aquinas

Ave verum

Hail to you, true body sprung
From the Virgin Mary's womb;
The same that on the cross was hung
Bearing for us bitter doom.
You whose side was pierced and flowed,
Both with water and with blood;
Grant us of your flesh to taste
When we lie in death's embrace.

O kind, O loving one,
O sweet Jesu, Mary's Son.

Lord Jesus Christ, pierce my soul

Lord Jesus Christ, pierce my soul with your love so that I
may always long for you alone, who are the bread of angels
and the fulfilment of the soul's deepest desires. May my
heart always hunger and feed upon you, so that my soul
may be filled with the sweetness of your presence. May my
soul thirst for you, who are the source of life, wisdom,
knowledge, light and all the riches of God our Father. May
I always seek and find you, think upon you, speak to you
and do all things for the honour and glory of your holy
name. Be always my only hope, my peace, my refuge and
my help in whom my heart is rooted so that I may never be
separated from you.

St Bonaventure

Anima Christi

Soul of Christ, sanctify me,
Body of Christ, save me,
Blood of Christ, inebriate me,
Water from the side of Christ, wash me,
Passion of Christ, strengthen me.
O good Jesus, hear me,
Within your wounds hide me;
Let me not be separated from you.
From the malicious enemy defend me.
In the hour of my death call me
And bid me come to you,
That with your saints I may praise you
For ever and ever. Amen.

Act of spiritual communion (when unable to receive the sacrament)

My Jesus, I believe that you are truly present in the most
Blessed Sacrament. I love you above all things, and I desire
to possess you within my soul. Since I am unable now to
receive you sacramentally, come at least spiritually into
my heart. I embrace you as if you were already there,
and I unite myself wholly to you; never permit me to be
separated from you.

St Alphonsus

Meditation

The human mother suckles her child with her own milk,
but our precious mother Jesus can feed us with himself, and
he does this most constantly and tenderly by means of the
Blessed Sacrament, which is the precious food of true life.
And through all the sweet Sacraments he sustains us in the
fullness of mercy and grace.

The human mother can put her child tenderly to her
breast, but our tender mother, Jesus, can lead us intimately
into his blessed breast through the sweet open wound in his
side, and there give us a glimpse of the Godhead and the
joy of Heaven, with the inner certainty of eternal bliss.

Julian of Norwich

I give you thanks

I give you thanks,
Lord, holy Father, everlasting God.
In your great mercy,
and not because of my own merits,
you have fed me, a sinner and your unworthy servant,
with the precious body and blood of your Son,
our Lord Jesus Christ.

I pray that this holy communion
may not serve as my judgement and condemnation,
but as my forgiveness and salvation.

May it be my armour of faith
and shield of good purpose.
May it root out in me all vice and evil desires,
increase my love and patience,
humility and obedience,
and every virtue.

Make it a firm defence
against the wiles of all my enemies, seen and unseen,
while restraining all evil impulses of flesh and spirit.
May it help me to cleave to you, the one true God,
and bring me a blessed death when you call.

I beseech you to bring me, a sinner,
to that glorious feast where,
with your Son and Holy Spirit,
you are the true light of your holy ones,
their flawless blessedness,
everlasting joy,
and perfect happiness.
Through Christ our Lord. Amen.

St Thomas Aquinas

Love of the Heart of Jesus

Love of the Heart of Jesus, inflame my heart.
Charity of the Heart of Jesus, flow into my heart.

Strength of the Heart of Jesus, support my heart.
Mercy of the Heart of Jesus, pardon my heart.
Patience of the Heart of Jesus, grow not weary of my heart.
Kingdom of the Heart of Jesus, be in my heart.
Wisdom of the Heart of Jesus, teach my heart.
Will of the Heart of Jesus, guide my heart.
Zeal of the Heart of Jesus, consume my heart.
Immaculate Virgin Mary, pray for me to the Heart of Jesus.

The Lord of glory

The Lord of glory
(O wondrous story!)
Hath made His home within my breast:
Bowed down before Him,
My soul adore Him
Who 'neath Thy roof vouchsafes to rest.
Good Angels, aid me,
The God Who made me,
Who died to save me, is now my Guest:
Ah, softly sing Him
Sweet songs, and bring Him
Your burning love, your worship blest.
The Lord of Glory
(O wondrous story!)
Now dwells within my breast.

When daylight shineth,
When day declineth,
In storm and sun, abide with me:
In joy and gladness,
In pain and sadness,
O let me, Lord, be nigh to Thee.
Good Shepherd, feed me,
And guard and lead me
To Thy bright pastures beyond the sea,
To make in glory
(O wondrous story!)

One long Communion eternally.
When daylight shineth,
When day declineth,
O Lord, abide with me.

Jesus alone for my goal

Jesus alone for my Goal,
Jesus alone for my Master,
Jesus alone for my Model,
Jesus alone for Guide,
Jesus alone for Joy and Riches,
Jesus alone for my Friend.

St Bernadette

Jesus, long my soul's desired

Jesus, long my soul's desired,
Now at length possessed,
Close my loving heart enfolds Thee,
Thou its cherished Guest.
May each faculty within me
Glad Hosannas sing,
Homage for the gracious visit
Of my Lord and King.

Not such brightness bringeth morning
To the night-bound earth,
Not such freshness, showers waking
Flowers to new birth,
As the life, the warmth, the sunlight
Jesus brings to me,
All renewing and refreshing
With His charity.

I was nothing; Thou didst draw me
From oblivion dark,
And my mind Thou didst illumine
With divinest spark.

Thou wast born for me an Infant
In a stable poor,
Dying on the Cross in anguish
Didst all pain endure.

And still every hour bringeth
Fresh proofs of Thy care,
And today Thyself Thou givest,
Gift beyond compare.
O my soul's delight, my Jesus!
Welcome o'er and o'er!
Reign, O freely reign within me
King for everymore!

Stay with me, O stay, my Jesus,
From the morning light,
Stay with me till twilight shadows
Deepen into night:
Stay with me from life's bright morning
Till her shaded eve,
Friend, and King, and Master, Jesus,
All my love receive!

O living bread

O living bread, that came down from heaven to give life to
the world! O loving shepherd of our souls, from your
throne of glory whence, a 'hidden God', you pour out your
grace on families and peoples, we commend to you particularly the sick, the unhappy, the poor and all who beg for
food and employment, imploring for all and every one the
assistance of your providence; we commend to you the
families, so that they may be fruitful centres of Christian
life. May the abundance of your grace be poured out over
all.

Pope John XXIII

Meditation

Let us flee to our Lord and we shall be comforted. Let us touch him and we shall be made clean. Let us cleave to him and we shall be secure and safe from every kind of harm. Our courteous Lord wants us to feel as at home with him as the heart can conceive or the soul desire. But let us be careful not to treat this close friendship so casually that we forget courtesy. For while our Lord is utter homeliness, he is as courteous as he is homely, for he is true courtesy. And he wants the blessed creatures, who will be in heaven with him forever, to be like him in all things, for to be exactly like our Lord is our true salvation and our greatest bliss. If we do not know how we shall do all this, then let us request it from our Lord, and he will teach us, for it is his delight and his glory; blessed may he be!

Julian of Norwich

Our Father, may everything I do

Our Father, may everything I do begin with your inspira-
tion, continue with your help,
and reach perfection under your guidance.
With your loving care guide all my daily actions.
Help me to persevere with love and sincerity.
Teach me to judge wisely of the things of earth and to love
the things of Heaven.
Keep me in your presence and never let me be separated
from you.
Your Spirit made me your child, confident to call you
Father;
Make your love the foundation of my life.
And I ask this through Jesus your beloved Son. Amen.

15

Prayers for Different Occasions

Renewal of baptismal promises

Today I freely renew the promises of my Baptism, asking that I may be clothed in the garments of Christlikeness and that Jesus alone may be the Lord of my heart. As I take this blessed water I ask to be cleansed of all my sins and to be renewed in grace as a child of God.

I believe in all that the Christian faith teaches, I hope in the promise of eternal life and I desire to grow daily in the love of God and others.

May Christ form his own image in me, and may my Baptism come to completion in a life filled with the Spirit, a witness to others that Jesus brings healing, forgiveness and joy into our broken world.

Mary, my mother, form the image of Jesus within me and make me all his own.

My patron saints, whose name I received at my Baptism, pray for me.

Dearest Jesus, help me

Dearest Jesus, help me to spread your fragrance every-
 where I go.
Flood my soul with your spirit and life,
penetrate and possess my whole being so utterly
that all my life may be but a radiance of yours.
Shine through me, and be so in me, that everyone I come
 in contact with
may feel your presence in my soul.
May they look up and see no longer me, but only Jesus.
 Amen.

Cardinal Newman

Set me, Father, in the full radiance

Set me, Father, in the full radiance of the face of your Son
that I may catch his beauty, and by what I become
show all the world that Jesus is still living in his Church.
 Amen.

Hymn of the holy name of Jesus

O Jesus, it is sweet to remember you, true joy of the heart;
but sweeter than honey, sweeter than anything, is your
 presence.
It is the most delightful song, joyful to hear,
it is the sweetest thought, Jesus, Son of God.
You are the hope of the repentant, loving with the one
 who asks,
good to the one who seeks.
So how could one describe what it means to find you?
No spoken word can describe, no written word express,
only the one who has experienced it can believe
what it is to love Jesus.
O Jesus, be our joy, and one day be our eternal rest.
To you be the glory, now and for ever. Amen.

Heart of Jesus, think on me

Heart of Jesus, think on me.
Eyes of Jesus, look on me.
Face of Jesus, shine on me.
Hands of Jesus, bless me.
Feet of Jesus, guide me.
Arms of Jesus, hold me.
Body of Jesus, feed me.
Blood of Jesus, cleanse me.
Make me, Jesus, your own, here and in the world to
   come. Amen.

The Jesus prayer

Lord Jesus Christ, Son of God,
have mercy on me, a sinner.

For others

Hear me, Lord, on behalf of those who are dear to me,
All whom I have in mind at this moment.
Be near them in all their anxieties and all their worries.
Give them the help of your saving grace.
I commend them all with trustful confidence to your
   merciful love.
Remember, Lord, all who are mindful of me, all who have
   asked me to pray for them,
all who have been kind to me,
all whom I have wronged by ill will or misunderstanding.
Give us all grace to bear each other's faults and to share
   each other's burdens.
Have mercy on the souls of our loved ones who have
   gone before us,
Grant them eternal peace and happiness with you. Amen.

The divine praises

Blessed be God.
Blessed be his holy Name.
Blessed be Jesus Christ, true God and true Man.
Blessed be the Name of Jesus.
Blessed be His most Sacred Heart.
Blessed be His most Precious Blood.
Blessed be Jesus in the Most Holy Sacrament of the Altar.
Blessed be the Holy Spirit the Paraclete.
Blessed be the great Mother of God, Mary most holy.
Blessed be her holy and immaculate Conception.
Blessed be her glorious Assumption.
Blessed be the name of Mary, Virgin and Mother.
Blessed be St Joseph, her spouse most chaste.
Blessed be God in his Angels and in his Saints.

Prayer before a crucifix

Behold, O kind and most sweet Jesus, I cast myself on my knees in your sight, and with the most fervent desire of my soul, I pray and beseech you that you would impress upon my heart lively sentiments of faith, hope and charity, with a true repentance for my sins and a firm desire of amendment, while with deep affection and grief of soul I ponder within myself and mentally contemplate your five most precious wounds, having before my eyes that which David spoke in prophecy of you, O good Jesus: 'They pierced my hands and my feet; they have numbered all my bones.'

Acts of faith, hope and love

Lord, I believe in you: increase my faith.
I trust in you: strengthen my trust.
I love you: let me love you more and more.
I am sorry for my sins: deepen my sorrow.

I worship you as my first beginning,
I long for you as my last end,

I praise you as my constant helper,
and call on you as my loving protector.

Guide me by your wisdom,
correct me with your justice,
comfort me with your mercy,
protect me with your power.

I offer you, Lord, my thoughts: to be fixed on you;
my words: to have you for their theme;
my actions: to reflect my love for you;
my sufferings: to be endured for your greater glory.

I want to do what you ask of me:
in the way you ask,
for as long as you ask,
because you ask it.

Lord, enlighten my understanding,
strengthen my will,
purify my heart,
and make me holy.

Prayer to accept suffering when it comes

My great God, you have humbled yourself and have been
lifted up on the tree! Though I am not fit to ask you for
suffering as a gift, at least I will beg of you grace to meet
suffering well, when you in your love and wisdom bring it
upon me.

Let me bear pain, reproach, disappointment, slander,
anxiety, suspense, when it comes. I wish to bear insult
meekly and to return good for evil. I wish to humble myself
in all things and to be silent when I am ill used, and to be
patient when sorrow or pain are prolonged. And all for the
love of you and your cross, knowing that in this way I shall
gain the promise of this life and of the next. Amen.

Cardinal Newman

Prayer of abandonment

Father,
I abandon myself into your hands;
do with me what you will.
Whatever you may do, I thank you;
I am ready for all, I accept all.
Let only your will be done in me,
and in all your creatures.
I wish no more than this, O Lord.
Into your hands I commend my soul;
I offer it to you with all the love of my heart,
for I love you Lord,
and so need to give myself,
to surrender myself into your hands without reserve,
and with boundless confidence,
for you are my Father.

Charles de Foucauld

A prayer for priests

Lord Jesus, you have chosen your priests from among us and sent them out to proclaim your word and to act in your name. For so great a gift to your Church we give you praise and thanksgiving. We ask you to fill them with the fire of your love, that their ministry may reveal your presence in the Church. Since they are earthen vessels, we pray that your power may shine out through their weakness. In their afflictions let them never be crushed; in their doubts never despair; in temptation never be destroyed; in persecution never abandoned. Inspire them through prayer to live each day the mystery of your dying and rising. In times of weakness send them your Spirit, and help them to praise your heavenly Father and to pray for poor sinners. By the same Holy Spirit put your word on their lips and your love in their hearts, to bring good news to the poor and healing to the broken-hearted. And may the gift of Mary your mother to the disciple you loved, be your gift to every priest. Grant that she who formed you in your human image may form them in your divine image, by the power of your Spirit, to the glory of God the Father. Amen.

Prayer for patience in sickness

Heavenly Father, your Son accepted our sufferings to teach us the virtue of patience in human illness. Hear my prayer and help me in my sufferings. May I realise that you have chosen me to be a saint through my sufferings and that I am joined to Christ in his sufferings for the salvation of the world.

Show me the power of your loving care and restore my health if it be your will, that I may offer joyful thanks in your Church.

Direct my heart and body in the love of you and the patience of Christ. Help me, defend me from all evil and bring me safely to life everlasting.

Heavenly Father, your will be done. Amen.

Prayer for missionaries

O God, bless all those who have gone out to bring the
    message of the Gospel to other lands.
We place before you especially: those who have had to
    leave their families behind; those who have to
    struggle with a new language and with new ways of
    thought; those who face constant discouragement in
    situations in which no progress ever seems to be
    made.
Bless all those who preach in the villages, the towns and
    the cities.
Bless those who teach in schools and colleges.
Bless those who work in hospitals and among the sick.
Bless those who have laid their gifts of craftsmanship or
    administration on the altar of missionary service.
Help us at home never to forget them and always to pray
    for them.
And bring quickly the day when the knowledge of you
    will cover the earth as the waters cover the sea.
We pray this in the name of Jesus, who is Lord. Amen.
                        Society of Mill Hill Missionaries

Learning Christ

In all the events of life
teach me Lord to be sweet and gentle;
in disappointments, in the thoughtlessness of others,
in the insecurity of those I trusted, in the unfaithfulness of
those on whom I relied.
Let me put myself aside to think of the happiness of
others,
to hide my little pains and heartaches, so that I may be the
only one to suffer from them.
Teach me to profit from the suffering that comes across my
path.
Let me so use it that it may mellow me, not harden or
embitter me;
that it may make me patient, not irritable, broad in my
forgiveness,
not narrow, haughty and overbearing.
May no one be less good for having come within my
influence;
no one less pure, less true, less kind, less noble
for having been a fellow-traveller on our journey towards
eternal life.
As I go my rounds from one distraction to another
let me whisper from time to time a word of love to you.
May my life be lived in the supernatural, full of power for
good, strong in its purpose for good,
and strong in its purpose of sanctity. Amen.

Prayer of a poor beggar to Jesus

O Jesus, give me, I beg you, the bread of humility,
the bread of obedience, the bread of charity,
the bread of strength to break my will and to mould it to
yours,
the bread of interior mortification, the bread of detach-
ment from creatures,
the bread of patience to bear the suffering my heart
endures.

O Jesus, you want me to be crucified, *Fiat.*
The bread to suffer as I ought, the bread of seeing you
alone in all things at all times.
Jesus, Mary, the Cross, I want no other friends but these.

St Bernadette

Prayer of St Richard of Chichester

Thanks be to you my Lord Jesus Christ,
for all the blessings which you have given to me,
all the sufferings you have borne for me.
O most merciful Friend, Brother and Redeemer,
may I know you more clearly, love you more dearly,
follow you more nearly,
day by day. Amen.

Meditation on providence

My God, you have created me to do some definite
service.
You have given some definite work to me which has been
given to no other.
I have my place in your plan.
I may never know what it is in this life but I will be told it
in the next.
Therefore I will trust you in all things.
If I am sick, my sickness may serve you.
If I am worried, my worry may serve you.
If I am in sorrow, my sorrow may serve you.
You do nothing in vain, you know what you are doing.
You may take away my friends, you may put me among
strangers,
You may make me feel forgotten; you may make my spirits
sink.
You may hide my future from me.
Still you know what you are doing and I trust you. Amen.

Cardinal Newman

Prayer of dedication to Christ

Lord Jesus Christ,
take all my freedom, my memory, my understanding, my
    entire will.
All that I have you have given to me,
I surrender it back to you to be guided only by your will.
Give me only your grace and your love, they are enough
    for me,
and with them I can want nothing more. Amen.

Prayer for a generous spirit

Dearest Jesus, teach me to be generous, to love you as
    you deserve to be loved,
to give and not to count the cost, to fight and not to heed
    the wounds,
to toil and not to seek for rest, to labour and not to ask for
    any reward,
except that of knowing that I do your will. Amen.

Prayer of St Francis

Lord, make me an instrument of your peace.
Where there is hatred, let me sow love;
where there is injury, pardon;
where there is doubt, faith;
where there is despair, hope;
where there is darkness, light;
where there is sadness, joy.
O divine Master, grant that I may not so much seek
to be consoled as to console,
to be understood as to understand,
to be loved as to love.
For it is in giving that we receive,
it is in pardoning that we are pardoned,
and in dying that we are born to eternal life. Amen.

Fill us with your love

Fill us with your love in the morning
and we will live the whole day in joy and praise.
Lord, listen to us.

Let my prayer rise before you like incense,
and my hands like the evening offering.
Lord, listen to us.

Restore sight to the blind;
straighten those who are bent.
Lord, listen to us.

Protect the weak and the needy;
support the widow and the orphan.
Lord, listen to us.

Come and cure all broken hearts;
give justice to the oppressed.
Lord, listen to us.

Give bread to the hungry;
give freedom to prisoners.
Lord, listen to us.

May your eternal Kingdom be ours;
give salvation to those who love you.
Lord, listen to us.

Based on Pss. 90:14; 141:2; 146:7–9

God be in my head

God be in my head and in my understanding.
God be in mine eyes and in my looking.
God be in my mouth and in my speaking.
God be in my heart and in my thinking.
God be at my end and at my departing.

Praise of the Lord God the Most High

You are the holy Lord, the only God who works wonders (Ps. 76:15).

You are strong, you are great, you are most high.

You are the Almighty King, heavenly Father, Lord of heaven and earth.

You are three and one, the Lord God of gods.

You are good, all good, the highest good, Lord God, living and true.

You are love, charity. You are wisdom, you are humility.

You are patience, you are beauty, you are meekness, you are security.

You are quietude, you are joy. You are our hope and gladness.

You are justice, you are temperance, you are our riches to the full.

You are beauty, you are meekness, you are our protector.

You are our guardian and defender; you are strength, you are refreshment.

You are our hope, you are our faith, you are our charity.

You are our deliverer, our delight, our eternal life,

the great and wondrous Lord, God Almighty, merciful Saviour. Amen.

St Francis of Assisi

Prayer to St Joseph

Saint Joseph, I humbly invoke you and commend myself and all who are dear to me to your intercession. By the love you have for Jesus and Mary do not abandon me during life and assist me at the hour of my death.

Loving St Joseph, faithful follower of Jesus Christ, I raise my heart to you to implore your powerful intercession in obtaining from the heart of Jesus all the graces necessary for my spiritual and temporal welfare, particularly the grace of a happy death. Be my guide, my father and my model through life, that I may merit to die as you did in the arms of Jesus and Mary. Amen.

Prayer in honour of St Joseph

God our Father, in every age you call men and women to develop and use their gifts for the good of others. With St Joseph as our example and guide, help us to do the work you have given us. Help those who are unemployed to use their talents in your service and to find work. May we all come to the rewards you have promised. We ask this through Christ our Lord. Amen.

Prayer in honour of St Therese

Eternal Father, whose infinite love watches in wisdom over each day of my life; grant me the light to see in sorrow as in joy, in trial as in peace, in uncertainty as in confidence, the way your divine Providence has marked for me. Give me that faith and trust in your care for me which was so pleasing to you in St Therese of the Child Jesus, and I will walk in darkness as in light, holding your hand and finding in all the blessings I receive from your loving bounty that everything is a grace. Amen.

Just for today

Lord, for tomorrow and its needs
   I do not pray;
Keep me, my God, from stain or sin,
   Just for today.

Let me both diligently work,
   And duly pray,
Let me be kind in word and deed,
   Just for today.

Let me be slow to do my will,
   Prompt to obey;
Help me to mortify my flesh,
   Just for today.

Let me no wrong or idle word
    Unthinking say;
Set Thou a seal upon my lips,
    Just for today.

Let me in season, Lord, be grave,
    In season gay;
Let me be faithful to Thy grace,
    Just for today.

And if today my tide of life
    Should ebb away,
Give me Thy Sacraments divine,
    Sweet Lord, today.

In Thine own dread but cleansing fires
    Brief be my stay;
Oh, bid me, if today I die,
    Go home today.

So, for tomorrow and its needs,
    I do not pray;
But keep me, guide me, love me, Lord,
    Just for today.

An evening prayer

May the Lord support us all the day long,
till the shades lengthen and the evening comes,
and the busy world is hushed and the fever of life is done.
Then in his mercy may he give us a safe lodging and a
    holy rest,
and peace at the last. Amen.

Night prayer

Watch, dear Lord, with those who wake or watch or weep
    tonight,
and give your angels charge over those who sleep.
Tend your sick ones, O Lord Christ,
rest your weary ones, bless your dying ones,
soothe your suffering ones, shield your joyous ones,
and all for your love's sake. Amen.

St Augustine

Litany of the Holy Name of Jesus

Lord, have mercy on us.
    Lord, have mercy on us.
Christ, have mercy on us.
    Christ, have mercy on us.
Lord, have mercy on us.
    Lord, have mercy on us.
Jesus, hear us.
    Jesus, graciously hear us.
God the Father of heaven,
    have mercy on us.
God the Son, redeemer of the world,
    have mercy on us.
God the Holy Spirit,
    have mercy on us.
Holy Trinity, one God,
    have mercy on us.
Jesus, Son of the living God,
    have mercy on us,
Jesus, splendour of the Father,
    have mercy on us.

Jesus, brightness of eternal light,
have mercy on us.
Jesus, king of glory,
have mercy on us.
Jesus, Son of justice,
have mercy on us.
Jesus, Son of the Virgin Mary,
have mercy on us.
Jesus, most amiable,
have mercy on us.
Jesus, most admirable,
have mercy on us.
Jesus, mighty God,
have mercy on us.
Jesus, father of the world to come,
have mercy on us.
Jesus, angel of great counsel,
have mercy on us.
Jesus, most powerful,
have mercy on us.
Jesus, most patient,
have mercy on us.
Jesus, most obedient,
have mercy on us.
Jesus, meek and humble of heart,
have mercy on us.
Jesus, lover of purity,
have mercy on us.
Jesus, lover of us,
have mercy on us.
Jesus, author of life,
have mercy on us.
Jesus, perfection of all virtues,
have mercy on us.
Jesus, zealous lover of souls,
have mercy on us.
Jesus, our refuge,
have mercy on us.
Jesus, father of the poor,
have mercy on us.

Jesus, treasure of the faithful,
have mercy on us.
Jesus, good shepherd,
have mercy on us.
Jesus, true light,
have mercy on us.
Jesus, eternal wisdom,
have mercy on us.
Jesus, infinite goodness,
have mercy on us.
Jesus, our way and our life,
have mercy on us.
Jesus, joy of angels,
have mercy on us.
Jesus, king of patriarchs,
have mercy on us.
Jesus, master of the apostles,
have mercy on us.
Jesus, teacher of the evangelists,
have mercy on us.
Jesus, strength of martyrs,
have mercy on us.
Jesus, light of confessors,
have mercy on us.
Jesus, purity of virgins,
have mercy on us.
Jesus, crown of all saints,
have mercy on us.
Be merciful unto us,
Jesus, spare us.
Be merciful unto us,
Jesus spare us.
From all evil,
Jesus, deliver us.
From all sin,
Jesus, deliver us.
From your wrath,
Jesus, deliver us.
From the snares of the devil,
Jesus, deliver us.

From everlasting death,
Jesus, deliver us.
From our failure to follow your inspiration,
Jesus, deliver us.
Through the mystery of your holy incarnation,
Jesus, deliver us.
Through your nativity,
Jesus, deliver us.
Through your infancy,
Jesus, deliver us.
Through your most divine life,
Jesus, deliver us.
Through your labours,
Jesus, deliver us.
Through your agony and passion,
Jesus, deliver us.
Through your cross and abandonment,
Jesus, deliver us.
Through your death and burial,
Jesus, deliver us.
Through your resurrection,
Jesus, deliver us.
Through your ascension,
Jesus, deliver us.
Through your reign in heaven,
Jesus, deliver us.
Through your joys,
Jesus, deliver us.
Through your glory,
Jesus, deliver us.
Lamb of God, you take away the sins of the world.
Spare us, O Jesus.
Lamb of God, you take away the sins of the world.
Graciously hear us, O Jesus.
Lamb of God, you take away the sins of the world.
Jesus, graciously hear us.

Let us pray

Lord Jesus Christ, who has said: 'Ask, and you shall receive; seek, and you shall find; knock, and it shall be opened unto you'; mercifully listen to our prayers and grant us the gift of your divine mercy, that we may ever love you with our whole heart and never cease from praising and glorifying your holy name. Give us, O Lord, a perpetual love of your holy name; for you never cease to be with those whom you establish in your love; who live and reign, world without end. Amen.

16

Hymns

O esca viatorum

O food of travellers, angels' bread,
Manna wherewith the blest are fed,
Come nigh, and with thy sweetness fill
The hungry hearts that seek thee still.

O fount of love, O well unpriced,
Outpouring from the heart of Christ,
Give us to drink of very thee,
And all we pray shall answered be.

And bring us to that time and place
When this thy dear and veilèd face
Blissful and glorious shall be seen –
Ah Jesu! – with no veil between.

Pange, lingua, gloriosi

Of the glorious body telling,
O my tongue, its mysteries sing,
And the blood, all price excelling,
Which the world's eternal king,
In a noble womb once dwelling,
Shed for this world's ransoming.

Given for us, for us descending,
Of a virgin to proceed,
Man with man in converse blending,
Scattered he the Gospel seed,
Till his sojourn drew to ending,
Which he closed in wondrous deed.

At the last great supper lying
Circled by his brethren band,
Meekly with the law complying,
First he finished its command,
Then, immortal food supplying,
Gave himself with his own hand.

Word made flesh, by word he maketh
Very bread his flesh to be;
Man in wine Christ's blood partaketh:
And if senses fail to see,
Faith alone the true heart waketh
To behold the mystery.

Therefore we, before him bending,
This great sacrament revere;
Types and shadows have their ending,
For the newer rite is here;
Faith, our outward sense befriending,
Makes the inward vision clear.

Glory let us give, and blessing
To the Father, and the Son;
Honour, might, and praise addressing,
While eternal ages run;
Ever too his love confessing,
Who, from both, with both is one.

Jesus, my Lord, my God, my all

Jesus, my Lord, my God, my all,
How can I love Thee as I ought?
And how revere this wondrous gift,
So far surpassing hope or thought?
      Sweet Sacrament, we Thee adore,
      O make us love Thee more and more.

Had I but Mary's sinless heart
To love Thee with, my dearest King,
O with what bursts of fervent praise
Thy goodness, Jesus, would I sing.
Sweet Sacrament, etc.

Ah see, within a creature's hand
The vast Creator deigns to be,
Reposing, infant-like, as though
On Joseph's arm, or Mary's knee.
Sweet Sacrament, etc.

Thy Body, Soul and Godhead, all,
O mystery of Love Divine,
I cannot compass all I have,
For all Thou hast and art are mine.
Sweet Sacrament, etc.

Sound, sound His praises higher still,
And come, ye Angels, to our aid,
'Tis God, 'tis God, the very God,
Whose power both man and Angels made.
Sweet Sacrament, etc.

O Jesus Christ, remember

O Jesus Christ, remember.
When thou shalt come again,
Upon the clouds of heaven,
With all thy shining train –
When every eye shall see thee
In deity revealed,
Who now upon this altar
In silence art concealed –

Remember then, O Saviour,
I supplicate of thee,
That here I bowed before thee
Upon my bended knee;
That here I owned thy presence,
And did not thee deny,
And glorified thy greatness
Though hid from human eye.

Accept, divine Redeemer,
The homage of my praise;
Be thou the light and honour
And glory of my days.
Be thou my consolation
When death is drawing nigh;
Be thou my only treasure
Through all eternity.

Sweet Sacrament Divine

Sweet Sacrament Divine,
Hid in Thine earthly home,
Lo, round Thy lowly shrine,
With suppliant hearts we come;
Jesus, to Thee our voice we raise,
In songs of love and heartfelt praise,
    Sweet Sacrament Divine.

Sweet Sacrament of Peace,
Dear Home of every heart,
Where restless yearnings cease,
And sorrows all depart;
There in Thine ear, all trustfully,
We tell our tale of misery,
    Sweet Sacrament of Peace.

Sweet Sacrament of Rest,
Ark from the ocean's roar,
Within Thy shelter blest,
Soon may we reach the shore.
Save us, for still the tempest raves,
Save lest we sink beneath the waves,
  Sweet Sacrament of Rest.

Sweet Sacrament Divine,
Earth's Light and Jubilee,
In Thy far depths doth shine
Thy Godhead's Majesty:
Sweet Light, so shine on us, we pray
That earthly joys may fade away,
  Sweet Sacrament Divine.

O Bread of Heaven, beneath this veil

O Bread of Heaven, beneath this veil
Thou dost my very God conceal:
My Jesus, dearest Treasure, hail;
I love Thee, and adoring kneel;
Each loving soul by Thee is fed
  With Thine own self in form of bread.

O Food of Life, Thou Who dost give
The pledge of immortality;
I live; no, 'tis not I that live;
God gives me life, God lives in me:
He feeds my soul, He guides my ways,
  And every grief with joy repays.

O Bond of love, that dost unite
The servant to his living Lord;
Could I dare live, and not requite
Such love, – then death were meet reward:
I cannot live unless to prove
  Some love for such unmeasured love.

Belovèd Lord, in Heaven above,
There, Jesus, Thou awaitest me;
To gaze on Thee with changeless love;
Yes, thus I hope, thus shall it be:
For how can He deny me Heaven
      Who here on earth Himself hath given?

Hail, Thou Living Bread of Heaven

Hail, Thou Living Bread of Heaven,
Sacrament of awful might:
I adore Thee, I adore Thee,
Every moment, day and night.

Heart, from Mary's heart created;
Heart of Jesus, all Divine,
Here before Thee I adore Thee,
All my heart and soul are Thine.

Soul of my Saviour, sanctify my breast

Soul of my Saviour, sanctify my breast;
Body of Christ, be Thou my saving Guest;
Blood of my Saviour, bathe me in Thy tide;
Wash me, ye waters, gushing from His Side.

Strength and protection may His Passion be,
O Blessed Jesus, hear and answer me,
Deep in Thy Wounds, Lord, hide and shelter me,
So shall I never, never part from Thee.

Guard and defend me from the foe malign.
In death's dread moments make me only Thine;
Call me, and bid me come to Thee on high,
Where I may praise Thee, with Thy Saints for aye.

I lift my heart to Thee

I lift my heart to Thee,
Saviour Divine,
For Thou art all to me,
And I am Thine.
Is there on earth a closer bond than this –
That Jesus Christ is mine, and I am His?

Thine am I by all ties,
But chiefly Thine
That through Thy Sacrifice
Thou, Lord, art mine.
By Thine own cords of love, so sweetly wound
About me, I to Thee am closely bound.

To Thee, Thou bleeding Lamb,
I all things owe,
All that I have, and am,
All that I know.
All that I have is now no longer mine,
And I am not mine own, Lord, I am Thine.

How can I, Lord, withhold
Life's brightest hour
From Thee, or gathered gold,
Or any power?
Why should I keep one precious thing from Thee
When Thou hast given Thine own sweet self for me?

I pray Thee, Jesus, keep
Me in Thy love,
And in death's holy sleep
Call me above
To that fair realm where, sin and sorrow o'er,
Thou and Thine own are one for evermore.

To Christ, the prince of peace

To Christ, the prince of peace,
And Son of God most high,
The father of the world to come,
Sing we with holy joy.

Deep in his heart for us
The wound of love he bore;
That love wherewith he still inflames
The hearts that him adore.

O Jesu, victim blest,
What else but love divine
Could thee constrain to open thus
That sacred heart of thine?

O fount of endless life,
O spring of water clear,
O flame celestial, cleansing all
Who unto thee draw near!

Hide us in thy dear heart,
For thither do we fly;
There seek thy grace through life, in death
Thine immortality.

Praise to the Father be,
And sole-begotten Son;
Praise, holy Paraclete, to thee
While endless ages run.

Adoro te devote

O Godhead hid, devoutly I adore thee,
Who truly art within the forms before me;
To thee my heart I bow with bended knee,
As failing quite in contemplating thee.

Sight, touch, and taste in thee are each deceived;
The ear alone most safely is believed:
I believe all the Son of God has spoken,
Than truth's own word there is no truer token.

God only on the cross lay hid from view;
But here lies hid at once the manhood too;
And I, in both professing my belief,
Make the same prayer as the repentant thief.

Thy wounds, as Thomas saw, I do not see;
Yet thee confess my Lord and God to be;
Make me believe thee ever more and more;
In thee my hope, in thee my love to store.

O thou memorial of our Lord's own dying!
O bread that living art and vivifying!
Make ever thou my soul on thee to live;
Ever a taste of heavenly sweetness give.

O loving Pelican! O Jesus, Lord!
Unclean I am, but cleanse me in thy blood;
Of which a single drop, for sinners spilt,
Is ransom for a world's entire guilt.

Jesus, whom for the present veiled I see,
What I so thirst for, oh, vouchsafe to me:
That I may see thy countenance unfolding,
And may be blest thy glory in beholding.

Mother, the King, my Lord and thine

Mother, the King, my Lord and thine,
Has made my heart His resting-place,
And well thou knowest that my breast
Is no fit home for such a guest.
How may I stand before His Face,
Knowing my weakness and disgrace
Unless I feel thy hand in mine,
    O Mother Mary?

With thine own mantle cover me,
Lend me the jewels thou dost wear,
That clinging trust no storm could shake,
That love which made thy true heart break,
Thy deep and self-effacing prayer,
Thy willingness His griefs to share,
So shall He find me like to thee –
    O Mother Mary.

Whether He comes with joy and peace,
Or brings His own dear gift of pain,
Help me to give Him welcome meet,
His coming with brave smile to greet.
If thou but aid me, not in vain
Will be my hope His Heart to gain,
And in His Love, thine shall increase,
    O Mother Mary.

Keep in my heart all through the day
The thought of Him like sweetest song,
And though that heart should hotly throb,
Watch that no hurt my peace may rob.
Win me the victory over wrong,
Teach me to suffer and be strong;
From Him and thee, let me not stray,
    O Mother Mary.

Sing of Mary, pure and lowly

Sing of Mary, pure and lowly,
Virgin-Mother undefiled.
Sing of God's own Son most holy,
Who became her little child.
Fairest child of fairest Mother,
God the Lord who came to earth,
Word made Flesh, our very Brother,
Takes our nature by His birth.

Sing of Jesus, Son of Mary,
In the home at Nazareth,
Toil and labour cannot weary
Love enduring unto death.
Constant was the love He gave her,
Though it drove Him from her side,
Forth to preach, and heal, and suffer,
Till on Calvary He died.

Sing of Mary, sing of Jesus,
Holy Mother's holier Son.
From His throne in heaven He sees us,
Thither calls us every one
Where He welcomes home His Mother
To a place at His right hand,
There His faithful servants gather,
There the crownèd victors stand.

Joyful Mother, full of gladness,
In thine arms thy Lord was borne,
Mournful Mother, full of sadness,
All thy heart with pain was torn.
Glorious Mother, now rewarded
With a crown at Jesus' hand,
Age to age thy name recorded
Shall be blest in every land.

Hail, Queen of Heav'n, the ocean Star

Hail, Queen of Heav'n, the ocean Star,
Guide of the wanderer here below,
Thrown on life's surge, we claim thy care,
Save us from peril and from woe.
Mother of Christ, Star of the sea,
Pray for the wanderer, pray for me.

O gentle, chaste, and spotless Maid,
We sinners make our prayer through thee,
Remind thy Son that He has paid
The price of our iniquity.
Virgin most pure, Star of the sea,
Pray for the sinner, pray for me.

Sojourners in this vale of tears,
To thee, blest advocate, we cry;
Pity our sorrows, calm our fears,
And soothe with hope our misery.
Refuge in grief, Star of the sea,
Pray for the mourner, pray for me.

And while to Him Who reigns above,
In Godhead One, in Persons Three,
The Source of Life, of Grace, of Love,
Homage we pay on bended knee,
Do thou, bright Queen, Star of the sea,
Pray for thy children, pray for me.

Ave Maria, thou Virgin and Mother

Ave Maria, thou Virgin and Mother,
Fondly thy children are calling to thee;
Thine are the graces unclaimed by another,
Sinless and beautiful Star of the Sea!

Ave Maria, the night shades are falling,
Softly our voices arise unto thee;
Earth's lonely exiles for succour are calling,
Sinless and beautiful Star of the Sea!

Ave Maria, thy children are kneeling –
Words of endearment are whispered to thee;
Softly thy spirit upon us is stealing,
Sinless and beautiful Star of the Sea!

Ave Maria, thy arms are extending,
Gladly within them for shelter we flee,
Are thy sweet eyes on thy lonely ones bending?
Sinless and beautiful – Star of the Sea!

In splendour arrayed

In splendour arrayed,
In vesture of gold,
The Mother of God
In glory behold!
O daughter of David,
Thou dwellest on high,
Excelling in brightness
The hosts of the sky.

O Maiden thou art
A Mother renowned;
A mother who yet
As virgin art crowned;
The Lord of the angels,
God high and supreme,
Took flesh of thy substance,
The world to redeem.

All kindreds and tongues
Thine offspring adore,
Creation must bow
His footstool before;
At thy gentle pleadings
May he from his height
Disperse all our shadows
And fill us with light.

The Father we praise,
Who chose for his Son
A Mother all-pure,
Th' immaculate one.
All praise to her offspring
Who saveth our race:
Like to the Spirit,
Who filled her with grace.

Mary immaculate, star of the morning

Mary immaculate, star of the morning,
Chosen before the creation began,
Chosen to bring, for thy bridal adorning,
Woe to the serpent and rescue to man.

Here, in an orbit of shadow and sadness
Veiling thy splendour, thy course thou hast run;
Now thou art throned in all glory and gladness,
Crowned by the hand of thy Saviour and Son.

Sinners, we worship thy sinless perfection;
Fallen and weak, for thy pity we plead;
Grant us the shield of thy sovereign protection,
Measure thine aid by the depth of our need.

Frail is our nature, and strict our probation,
Watchful the foe that would lure us to wrong.
Succour our souls in the hour of temptation,
Mary immaculate, tender and strong.

See how the wiles of the serpent assail us,
See how we waver and flinch in the fight;
Let thine immaculate merit avail us,
Make of our weakness a proof of thy might.

Bend from thy throne at the voice of our crying,
Bend to this earth which thy footsteps have trod;
Stretch out thine arms to us living and dying,
Mary immaculate, mother of God.

Sei pura, sei pia

O Mother blest, whom God bestows
On sinners and on just,
What joy, what hope thou givest those
Who in thy mercy trust.

Thou art clement, thou art chaste,
Mary, thou art fair;
Of all mothers sweetest, best;
None with thee compare.

O heavenly mother, mistress sweet!
It never yet was told
That suppliant sinner left thy feet
Unpitied, unconsoled.

O mother pitiful and mild,
Cease not to pray for me;
For I do love thee as a child,
And sigh for love of thee.

Most powerful mother, all men know
Thy Son denies thee nought;
Thou askest, wishest it, and lo!
His power thy will hath wrought.

O mother blest, for me obtain,
Ungrateful though I be,
To love that God who first could deign
To show such love for me.

Jesus, the dying day hath left us lonely

Jesus, the dying day hath left us lonely:
All fadeth from us, Thou remainest only:
Earth's light goes out, but Thou, True Light, art near us,
  And Thou wilt hear us.

Bring home the feet that far from Thee have wandered;
The minds that all but Thee all day have pondered;
We yield them evermore, awake or sleeping,
  To Thy safe keeping.

O let our souls keep day, though night be round us,
So shall the sons of darkness not confound us,
But blameless rest delight Thy gaze paternal,
  Untired Eternal.

White Dove of Peace, Great God of consolation,
Brood o'er the souls that sigh in tribulation,
And with the whisper of serene tomorrows,
  Soothe all their sorrows.

Mother of Holy Hope, all-Blessèd Mary,
Whose high-throned Mother-love can never vary,
This night, and at our death's deep nightfall aid us,
  With Him Who made us.

Sweet Saviour, bless us ere we go

Sweet Saviour, bless us ere we go;
Thy word into our minds instil;
And make our lukewarm hearts to glow
With lowly love and fervent will.

Through life's long day and death's dark night,
O gentle Jesus, be our light.

The day is done; its hours have run;
And thou hast taken count of all,
The scanty triumphs grace has won,
The broken vow, the frequent fall.

Grant us, dear Lord, from evil ways
True absolution and release;
And bless us more than in past days
With purity and inward peace.

Do more than pardon; give us joy,
Sweet fear and sober liberty,
And loving hearts without alloy,
That only long to be like thee.

Labour is sweet, for thou has toiled,
And care is light, for thou hast cared;
Let not our works with self be soiled,
Nor in unsimple ways ensnared.

For all we love – the poor, the sad,
The sinful – unto thee we call;
Oh let thy mercy make us glad;
Thou art our Jesus and our all.